OUT SIDERS

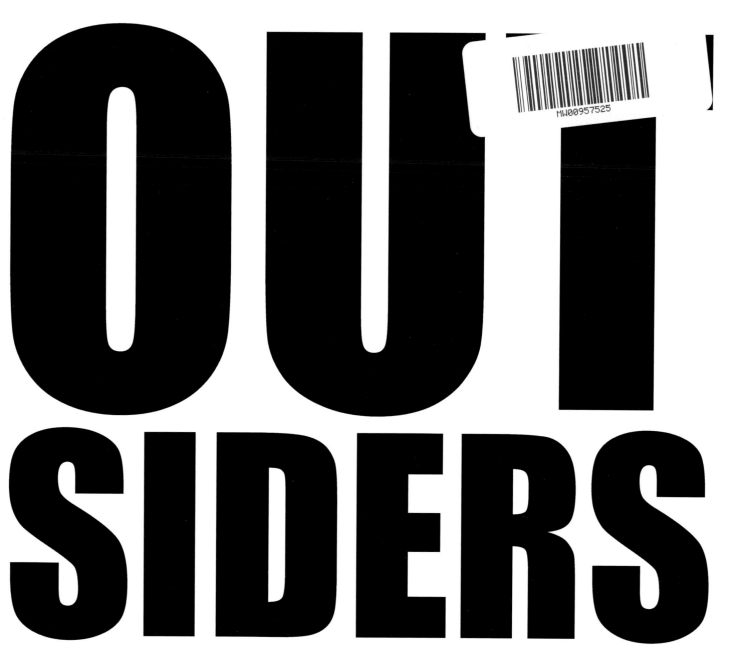

Not One Of Us:
Interviews with the unique,
extraordinary and misunderstood

ISBN-13: 978-1475246476
ISBN-10: 1475246471

www.gazcook.com
www.lovetown.eu

Inside

Garry Cook, 37. Not photographed

A journalist and photographer, this is his book. This collection of interviews is intended to explore what it means to be an Outsider. The profiles cover some vastly diverse subjects. The intention is to examine how people are judged. There has been an attempt to do this without bias or comment. However, from inception to completion, the photographer's decisions have shaped this book.

"Are you scared of the local hoodies? Believe the BNP are a bunch of Nazi racists? Do you look at homeless people and think, 'lazy bastards'? Perhaps you hate religion? Maybe you presume sadomasochists are perverted?

Are you suspicious of women wearing hijabs? Are you a racist? Could you survive if you were homeless? Do you know the name of your local vicar? Are you too scared to realise your sexual fantasies?

Do you judge people by the way they look?

We judge people constantly. People in the street, people at work, people on TV, people in the pub. It's natural. Nowt wrong with that actually. But what if you're wrong? What if your prejudice leaves the victim of your stares feeling isolated? We all judge people on first impressions. Sometimes we're right, sometimes we're not.

With these profiles I'm hoping you will question your judgements about people by looking at their photo and then reading their story.

What is my point of view? As far as this book is concerned – and without wanting to put ideas into your head – this book is about freedom of speech and judging others.

Freedom of speech because there are some subjects which aren't allowed to be discussed fairly and openly. Some subjects are taboo to the point that most people are unable to have an informed opinion about them. The media has a lot to answer for in this respect.

They have shaped opinion on some emotive subjects without fully informing their readers and without their readers realising it, and I include myself as one of the influenced. Just because a subject is difficult does not mean it should be misrepresented.

As for judging, well, people come in all sorts of shapes and sizes, with all kinds of baggage and backgrounds. We are harsh judges of those we don't know. You can only judge someone on their actions, but just as they are responsible for their own actions, we are responsible for our own judgements. Or we should be.

If you're going to judge someone, at least do it in an informed way – then you might just judge them differently.

All those profiled here are done so in direct quotes so my own opinions do not influence or distort what those interviewed are trying to say. Read the profiles, think, enjoy."

Photographs and text by Garry Cook © // e-mail: gazcook@hotmail.com

Ken, age unknown, speaker. Photographed in Hyde Park

In 1865 the Reform League was established to fight for rights of the working classes. The League held two meetings in Hyde Park in 1866 and 1867 despite massive police and military opposition. Hyde Park Corner has since been used as a platform for free speech on Sundays. Karl Marx, Vladimir Lenin and George Orwell have all held court at the venue.

 Rule 9: No violence. Rule 10: to ask a question raise your hand. All heckles must be funny. Rule 12a: No violence. Rule 15: No violence.

The oath of allegiance in schools? Load of bloody rubbish. We don't need no oath of allegiance. If they aren't in support of this country, send them back to Brazil where they come from.

That bastard in Pret A Manger this morning accused me of shoplifting a sandwich. I did not shoplift a sandwich from Pret A Manger. Why should I? I'd already eaten a sandwich I'd shoplifted from Costa Coffee. So why should I need to shoplift a sandwich from Pret A Manger? Brazilian bastard. Fuck off back to Brazil and take an oath of allegiance to Brazil when you get there. Stay in Brazil. Don't come over here working in Pret A Manger falsely accusing me of shoplifting.

Why are you all standing so far away? I mean come right up to me. It's allowed. Then I won't have to shout and it's more conversational.

Do you know about them hanging the monkey, have you heard of that? During the Napoleonic wars a warship ran aground at Hartlepool near Newcastle and all the sailors were killed. The only survivor was the ship's pet monkey and the silly Northerners thought he was a French spy so they hung him. That's Northerners for you.

You're a Southerner I take it. You are? Andrea. You are? Margo. Loren. Loren, I'm

Ken, nice to meet you. Have I told you about this girl here? Dani. She's 17 and she said, Ken, when I'm 18 I'm going to have sex with you. I said when's your 18th birthday?

But this year, if I haven't had her by the 31st of December, I'll not be happy. See what she makes of that, she'll probably like it.

Today is Palm Sunday. Next Sunday is Easter Sunday so we'll all be eating chocolate. Green and Blacks chocolate.

My four main subjects are Christianity, anarchism, veganism and existentialism. That's what I talk about the most. I actually have 116 subjects in my repertoire, but there are eleven that I specialise in. They are anarchism, Catholicism, Christianity, Church of England, draconian method, Ockham's Razor, tractarianism and then zoroastrianism. I do get a lot of dialogue. It's surprising the number of people who know who Ockham's Razor is and ask me. It is a test to see if I know what I'm talking about. But I've defined Ockham's Razor so many times over the past five or six months if I don't know what Ockham's Razor is by now I'm never going to.

Been doing this since 1993. I do it for the good of democracy. For the good of free speech for free speech's sake. Free speech because in 1866 blood was spilled. Heads were cracked and blood was spilled in the Hyde Park riot of 1866 to establish the right of free speech. So in honour of those people I believe it should be practiced. The big issue of the moment here is the situation in Iraq. Generally speaking on a

Sunday you get a review of the last six days' news.

Contemporary events are the biggest single issue here. Iraq, Afghanistan, that sort of thing, Darfur, whatever is the news subject of the moment. The American presidential election. The budget, all that sort of thing. There was a peace march yesterday.

I work at the Tate Gallery three days a week. It's therapeutic earnings as I'm on benefits. I'm allowed to work three times, eight hours without it affecting my benefits. They call it therapeutic earnings. Just a welcomer, standing inside the door. It's not particularly taxing work. But there's no tax. That's the thing about income tax. If there wasn't income tax there wouldn't be no government.

Not only are we oppressed but we're paying to be oppressed out of our own pockets. I do not approve of paying income tax. Income tax is what keeps the government in existence. If we didn't pay income tax the government would go bankrupt and they'd bugger off and leave us alone. And I would approve of that cos I'm an anarchist.

As you've probably worked out from what I've just said, I'm an anarchist. Even a five-year-old child could work out that I'm an anarchist.

That, I take it, is a tape recorder. It is a tape recorder?

Who's this then? That's a sight for sore eyes I haven't seen him in for months. Good afternoon Ron, how are you?

Carl Makovecz, 45, Reiki Master Teacher. Photographed in Manchester

Developed in 1922 by Japanese Buddhist Mikao Usui, Reiki – Rei meaning 'the wisdom of God' and Ki meaning 'life-force energy' – is a spiritualist treatment sometimes referred to as 'healing hands'. Makovecz is helped in his practice by several spirit guides, including a Samurai Warrior, a nun and Jesus Christ. He has travelled the world teaching Reiki. He works for a company which makes pool tables.

" It's holistic healing. I draw on universal life-force energy which is all around us. We all have a certain amount of healing energy within us. It's called Ki. It's what keeps us alive. But when you've been attuned you can just tap in and instead of just flowing through you, it's in abundance, it's inexhaustible.

I went to a spiritualist church and it was just picked out by a few mediums. They just kept telling me all the time, 'you've got to do healing'. So I thought, alright I'll look into this. Didn't know anything about it really. And then I recalled a dream I used to have as a small child. It was brought back to me again. And I thought, this is mad this. Why am I having this dream? As a child, and it was me walking around a hospital just laying my hands on people.

Then I started to see spirits from the spirit word. So I joined a clairvoyant class and started giving messages to people and it was just mind blowing. You just allowed whoever the spirit was to blend with you and they sort of moulded on to you and they put their mannerism on you. So I'm what – 5ft 8ins – and am like taking long strides and I said, 'I don't walk like this, I just don't walk like this'. I've got a very tall gentleman with me.

I knew certain guides who I had with me, that I could call upon, had made themselves known to other people, to other mediums. When I've been speaking you can just see the look on their face. They say, 'do you know you've got a Native American Indian stood at the back of you?' and I said yes, he's one of many guides. You come into this world with a guardian angel and a doorkeeper who are there to help, guide and protect you. I have quite a few healing guides.

I always place protection around myself and the room, I cleanse it before they come. And then I call him, the Christ energy, because I have the Christ energy working with me as well, Jesus Christ.

I woke up one morning, early Sunday morning. They show me things from time to time, the spirits. But you don't see them from here, you don't see them with these eyes. You see them from here – your third eye. I just sat up and I thought, what am I looking at? I just

sat up in bed and I thought I could see myself walking in the air but I'm looking up into the sky. And I thought what's going on? As I was looking up I could see this crucifix in the sky and this light around the top of the head of Christ. And the feeling, as I looked up, the feeling was just unbelievable. I've never had a feeling like it in my life. I had every emotion running through me, from happiness, sadness, joy. It was just, phewww, watching it… I, I, I was speechless. And I spoke to a good medium friend of mine and he said, 'wow, you've got the Christ energy working with you'.

While I was at a meeting at spiritualist church I was talking to one of the mediums outside. Another medium came out. This other medium says to me, 'can I just stop you, you've got a crucifix on your shoulder there, you've got the Christ energy with you'. I said yes I know. He said, 'it's amazing.'

I always call the Christ energy, Quan Yin. She's the eastern Goddess of Compassion. I'm sat there, sat relaxing, had some Reiki music on and out of the corner of my eye, this lady was stood here. As I was sat, on that side, she was just stood here. Just looking at me. So I'm literally five feet away. And I thought, someone's looking at me. And I just turned and looked and it was clear as I can see you now, it was as clear as I could see her. This Japanese lady Quan Yin in full kimono, big pink woolly flowers. Jet black hair. Awesome, she was absolutely gorgeous. And I'm just like, I couldn't speak. I didn't know who it was at the time. I just felt like I needed to be on my knees. I was just blown away. I was like that. Ahhh.

I did a couple of Reiki attunements and as I've gone in to get some water for one of the clients they are both sat in here and I've come back in and they've said, 'Carl, that was mind blowing'. They said, 'while you had your hands on me and then you moved down to my legs and my feet I knew where you were because I could feel you but then I felt a pair of hands come on my head'. They work through me and they use me as an instrument of love and it's awesome.

I have a Japanese Samurai healer. I have an African Zulu Warrior doorkeeper. He lets nobody in unless it's okay. He's the bouncer, if you like, in the spirit world for your body. So

it's alright, nobody can come in and cause mayhem. You have mental breakdowns if a lower entity spirit got in and caused havoc. He's there to prevent all that. Sister Anne, she's my Reiki guide. Native American Indian, not sure if he's called White Cloud. He's with me a lot. He works on the emotional side, if emotional healing is needed he comes. Quan Yin, she's there for everybody, compassion and all sorts. As well as the arch-angels, Raphael and other certain angels for whatever situation is needed. I have a healing list.

Everybody has a certain amount of healing to give. Everybody. They can all heal. But if you've not had the attunements for the Reiki, if you were to go around giving hugs and listening to people, talk about all their problems, and then you go home after doing that for six, seven, eight hours you would go home and say I'm knackered, I'm drained.

And all you've done is give your energy, the life-force energy that you have, to everybody else and you go home drained. But with the Reiki I could do that for 24/7 and not feel drained at all. Because when I tap into this energy it charges me up as well as you.

I don't get loads of people coming all the time otherwise I would look into stopping doing the pool tables. I'm just looking at different alleyways to go down to do, I want to do the Reiki full-time. It's where I'm being led.

Onoohra – I forgot a guide, he's just letting me know! – an Egyptian guide I've got.

No-one comes to Reiki for no reason. I've had quite a few women who've come with lots of emotional problems, whether it be partners, break-ups, divorces, whatever, anything like that. Half-way through a treatment I can go direct to a problem. They'll be crying. They'll be wailing on the bed, on my Reiki table in hysterics. I calm them down. I said, between you and me you've got plenty of emotional problems. The Reiki is helping you to release all your problems. These problems that you're having that you are releasing now are going back many years. You won't ever forget all the bad things that have ever happened in your life, they just won't be there to give you all the aggravation and the troubles and the problems in the future. The Reiki puts things into order and sorts them out. "

Ivan Mackerle, 66, treasure hunter. Photographed in Prague

Brought up under communist rule in the Czech Republic, Mackerle's dreams of exploration around the world remained largely unfulfilled – apart from a three-week trip to Scotland to search for the Loch Ness Monster – until Czechoslovakia divided into two states in 1993. Mackerle has since travelled the globe searching for strange creatures, mythical monsters – including a giant killer worm in Mongolia – and Nazi treasures. He drives a German Light Amphibious Volkswagen car.

" In the beginning it was curiosity about unsolved mysteries and then I found it was a very big adventure. We know we need very good luck to solve something. More often our expeditions are small results. We bring new informations but we cannot solve, we have no evidence. But it is a very good feeling to go on adventures because of the danger. Unfortunately we cannot take the car on our expeditions because we fly. I used to collect articles about mysteries and so on and then I asked myself if it is true or fantasy. I started to search if it contains truth.

My first trip was to Scotland to find the Loch Ness monster. It was a communist time. It was impossible to travel through the border. I asked our government many times. I was very angry and I wrote to the president. Finally they give me permission.

We went to Romania to search for Dracula. And then it was searching our Republic, for example I have big interest about Golem. They gave me permission to climb up into the attic of the Old-New Synagogue in Prague, because it is a forbidden place. Then we searched for treasures from the Second World War from Germans.

In Madagascar we searched for the Man Eating Tree. We wanted to spend the night near one big baobab tree about which the natives said, 'this tree eats victims'. It was an old, old tree. We were attacked by natives with spears. We went to our car and turned on the windows. They came after us with long white coats and spears they cried 'arghhhh!' at us. Our guide was Madagascan, he was scared to death and said, 'we must run away, it's too dangerous'. When we got away in this car they jump on this car. I see the face from 30cms through the glass. As we got more speed they jumped off. The natives were very aggressive.

We have with us one boy, a guide, from another group of natives, he told us it would be dangerous because this tribe attacked other people. They were very aggressive and they were very bitter in this area. This boy was 20 years old. His mother cried when we returned. When we wanted to find this place nobody wanted to go and show us this place. This boy wanted to have jeans. We gave him our jeans so he went with us for this gift, but his

mother told him, 'don't go, don't go'. When we returned, all night we had a tent in the centre of his village and the people sat around our tent all night, watching us. They told us the natives thought that white people want to fuck their women, so they were very aggressive to everybody who was white.

Two trips were the most successful. The first trip was to Mongolia, because until this time only Mongolians knows about this creature, this worm. In the West nobody knows about it. And we collect stories about it. In England Dr [Karl] Shuker is a very well known cryptologist and he called me about our expedition to see if I can give him some more information.

The second was to Siberia two years ago. I have every day e-mails from Russians. At the present time the Russians prepare a big expedition with scientists, helicopters. They search for Valley of Death, there are some strange cauldrons, some metal buildings, from an unknown material, it looks like a copper but is very hard. We took GPS positions of these places. I wrote in this article that there is something very strange, could be some geological anomaly. This is the reason why Russian scientists want to go. They ask me for the co-ordinates. We will see what they find.

We were afraid of bears in Siberia but we had this guide with a rifle. When I first heard of these cauldrons in Siberia I thought this is not true, it is impossible that these strange objects are in Siberia, no military, no soldiers, no Russians. It was only writing, no photos, pictures made by some eye witnesses.

When we went there I think that we won't find something. They say that these objects slowly submerged in the ground. And we found in this area some strange places, we used a pole to feel something hard. It could be metal but it could also be ice.

But there is one problem because this shaman said that in this Valley of Death that people who spent some time here near these cauldrons die of a horrible death, illness, some strange illness and then finally they die. I didn't believe it but on the second day after we spent the night near this pool there was also something spherical under the water, but only small in metres. We went to sleep near there and when I woke up I had big problems

with headache and balance. Very bad. The worm. Now I don't think that this creature is from flesh and blood. But I believe that it is something else. A mythical creature, a creature from another dimension. When people are in some mind state, special state of mind, you can see what in a normal state you cannot see. Our brain is so programmed that we see only what we need for our life. We tried to bring it to the surface. Explosives. We had small explosives, we smuggled them into Russia. Got them here in Czech on the black market. We took it with us in the luggage.

A shaman warned us that it is dangerous, what we want to do. The worm is a demon, not a creature of flesh and blood. And Mongolians are afraid. The shaman said, 'cursed, you will be cursed'. We thought we can do it. We spent the night in tents and I have a bad dream that this creature went up from the sand and I was frozen with fear. It jumped from the sand on to my back. And I felt very big pain and I cried and at this moment I woke up. I was lying in the tent and my friend next to me, a medical doctor, he asked me, 'why do you cry?'. I told him about it. The pain was still there. I took off my shirt to look at my back and I have under my skin blood – this blue bruising all over my back. Blood boils. We discussed it and what it means and I since think it could be a curse from this shaman. Because it was a secret place and there were people who did not want us there. My heart was fine, it was only under my skin.

We tried to explore mystery flights near one river on the border between India and Nepal. People told us that there all around is tigers. But when you read in books everyone says that tigers are not around at this present time. And when tourists want to go on safari nobody can take pictures because they are very shy. So we didn't believe people that there were tigers. And so when we went in the forest with a tent and we spent two nights. One morning we woke up and found near the tent the big tracks of a tiger. We were scared. The one big weapon against the tiger is fire. In morning at five o'clock it was dark. The fire was gone off and I prayed to God because I think that the tiger is near us – I heard the cracking of wood. We smell tiger, wild animals, it was very strong. "

Brian Pattila, 62, trainspotter. Photographed in Ramsbottom, Lancashire

Brought up in North-east England, Pattila developed a fascination for trains as a youngster in the 1950s. After his children were born he rekindled his passion for steam and diesel locomotives in the early 1980s, regularly visiting stations and travelling the country to see new engines.

" I was seven. We went to live with my grandma in Gateshead. There was a park and the line came past the park and if you climbed to the top of the slide you could get the number. That started me going. All the lads used to run up the top when they saw a train coming.

We used to go down every night and count them, get inside. You could see the engines out of the window. Oh, there's a streak in, what they called a streak – A4. Used to climb over the wall and get in them. I got nabbed once by the railway police. Got fined 7s 6d I think. Pleaded guilty by letter. I was eight or nine years old. My only dealing with the law that, from the wrong side.

Back in the 1950s there were lots of clubs used to organise coach trips. In the 50s there were lots of people standing together.

In our second life in the eighties we used to organise private trips in cars or sometimes in a mini bus on the odd occasion. We'd go to the shed and we'd always elect someone to go and ask the foreman if we could look round. By the time you'd asked you'd seen half of what there was there anyway, even if they said no you managed to write down about 15 numbers.

Even from the 80s to now a lot of the sheds have closed. Crewe shed's closed. Seeing ten trains in a day would be a good day now, but in the Sixties we used to see hundreds. I can remember being on a train when I was 13 and every engine I saw was brand new.

The most exciting thing is to see a train you've never seen before. [My friend] Pete is interested in the technical side of it because he drives them. Pounds per square inch and the size of the pistons and all that, but that doesn't interest me particularly.

Some of the older blokes now, they take the unit numbers of coaches or wagons. I've met blokes at Warrington making notes of all the wagons when they go past. I mean, that's a bit beyond me. I wouldn't want to go to that level. Each individual wagon containing coal or whatever, you know. That's just because they carry on doing what they do and there's no engines left so they just turn to something else to provide an interest.

For me [the enjoyment] is to see what I haven't seen before. You write it down when you're out and then rule them off when you get home. Whatever few engines there are I'll be there writing them down and when I get back I'll have a look in my book and see if I needed them.

I've just bought this year's book a few weeks back. It comes out every year. What I do is mark up the ones that I haven't seen and then I underline them to say I have seen them. I've got one so far this year when I was in Manchester Victoria a few weeks back, when I was waiting for the tram. That's all I've managed. It's very hard these days. I don't really go out purposely to go on a train journey – although I'm still hoping to do my Leeds journey in a few weeks.

I've spoken to youngsters who have started in the last few years and what they do, because there is not so many as there used to be, they collect them all and start again. Just because they like doing it.

When [my wife] Valerie went to New York, when she was 60 a few years back, I had a day out on my own at Crewe station. It was dead as a dodo, you know, but there was still about half a dozen blokes, mostly older than me, taking numbers, taking photographs. But the atmosphere has completely changed, even 20 years ago there would have been crowds on the platform. If you go back to the 50s and you see archive film, the platform is full of little kids, big kids and blokes, all crowding on the platform, writing numbers down and taking photographs. Talking to the engine driver or whatever. Now it is just a handful.

I like to go on railway journies. Other people like reading books or listening to music. I look out of the window to see all the engines go past. Or standing at the station or whatever, you know. It's exciting, to me anyway, and to lots of other as well.

My happiest train memory… probably the thing that comes to mind is when just me and [my daughter] Melanie went when she was eight or nine. Susan was only five so she was a bit young. And we sat on Euston Station and it was a glorious sunny day and I remember she was saying, 'oh, it's a trainspotters paradise'. That was Melanie's words. As I say, not that she was interested in trains per se but it was just the fact of sitting there in the sun eating your sandwiches, and your flask of coffee having had a three-hour journey on a train.

It was a day trip. We went early in the morning. Spent the day going round the Underground to different stations. It was great.

No sad moments watching trains. Even when it's bad it's still pretty good. I'm paraphrasing David Frost, he wrote that one. David Frost's definition of sex, in the Sixties, on his Frost programme, 'when it's good, it's pretty good. When it's bad, it's still pretty good'. Something like that, I'm probably misquoting him. But that's the same sort of thing, even the bad days are good.

Sometimes you go out and you come back soaking wet, you know, and you haven't really got very far, seen very many, but it's still a day out, isn't it? You meet people. Over the years I must have met thousands of people.

I've just looked into the timetable the other night. Because Valerie is going to Ireland with her friend for a few days so I thought I'll get the Leeds trip in then.

Part of what I like to do is travel on lines that I haven't been on. I also have an Atlas and I've marked off all the lines that I've travelled on. And I've never been round Leeds very much so part of my day is to travel on lines I've never been on before. Normally when you go to Leeds you go on the main line but there is also another line that goes through Hebden Bridge and Halifax.

With my rail pass I can get as far as Littleborough. Then I have to get a ticket from there to the next station in Yorkshire. And then I'm buying a Rover ticket in Yorkshire so it's costing me about £7.60 or something for the day. That's not bad, is it?

I've planned this trip so I can pass stations where there used to be lots of engines. Don't know what it's like now, but there was a place called Healey Mills that we used to go with Pete in the car. I'm just going to go past there and hope that I might see something.

It's just a day out. I'll be on my own but I'm sure I'll bump into various people.

I'll be travelling round most of the day. The biggest stay I've got in one place will be about 40 minutes while I wait for my train. I also like the atmosphere of the stations. "

Nick Griffin, 49, chairman of the British National Party. Photographed in Burnley

Once dismissively known as Britain's Nazi party, the BNP has a growing number of supporters across the country, particularly in areas with large multi-racial communities. The right-wing party is notorious for its views on immigration and has been accused of stirring up racial hatred in problem areas – working-class northern towns like Oldham and Burnley.

 The BNP, when I was elected to lead it, had about 1200 members. It's now got more than 10,000 and the idea that you can have a hidden agenda party when you are recruiting nine times your existing number to a respectable front, it's a nonsense – the party has genuinely changed.

In some areas, even new areas we go into, the phrase that comes back repeatedly over the years, is people treating you like liberators walking down the street and they say, 'where have you been?'. There's tremendous enthusiasm in some places. In others there's a guarded respect. And in others it's, 'you're not the National Front are you?', which is the most common thing. So there's nothing wrong with the BNP in ordinary people's eyes, it's just the concern of what's behind or in the past and have things really changed. The average person, politically-minded, will say, 'I agree with what you say' in policy terms and in terms of perception of [what] the problems in society are, 'but I don't agree with what you do'. When they say that, they are thinking about what they've seen on BBC docu-dramas where we go throwing bricks through Asian shop windows and nonsense like this.

In a population that has probably given up voting, certainly in local elections, to be perceived as different to the rest is potentially of enormous value. So we're in this strange half-way house between being reviled and detested in the way the left media say we are and regarded as the best things since sliced bread. Basically people agree with what we say but are concerned about the image.

The thing which we really are with most of people is, 'well, at least they tell the truth'. We may be a bit rough round the edges. We're a very small, under-funded, shambolic organisation in many ways, but because we've offered an alternative and have shown that in certain circumstances the public will vote for us, we've forced the entire political elite to at least pay lip-service to talking about the issues.

Trevor Philips and others have said, 'unless we talk about these issues then the BNP are the only ones talking about these issues and the public will switch to them'.

As a general rule whenever we are elected we actually make an impact, racial attacks by whites fall, which I put down to a community which believes that it is represented, that its concerns are represented in the political process, and doesn't have to go outside the political process. The liberals who say, 'oh, people vote for the BNP then racial attacks will rise' should know better.

At the moment we have a lack of or feeling that there's no chance of fair political representation. It's an open invitation to violence and, in the end, terrorism. If you can express theoretically unpopular minority views through the ballot box you don't have to go down the road and putting bricks through windows. So when you see racial attack rates falling in Barking and Dagenham after we got elected I'd say that bares out the logic of the position that if people think they are being represented they don't have to go and do anything else.

Yes, there is racial violence. Every single multi-cultural, multi-racial society in the world has racial violence, whether it's Kenya, Rwanda, Serbia or Britain. Throughout history most of the bloodiest conflicts are the same thing. Britain isn't immune. The more multi-cultural we are the more tensions, more stresses, the more violence there will be. That violence isn't created by people who recognise the differences. It's actually created by the liberals who try and gloss over the differences. To say that the people who warned that this system was going to cause trouble wanted it is like saying the weatherman is responsible for the storm. It's an illogical fallacy.

In certain areas, any of the mixed northern towns, someone who is second generation West Indian or half West Indian, half English, almost all identify with us and look up to us for help because their kids get picked on by young Muslims even more than our kids do. Likewise Sikhs don't like Hindus. There's not many Sikhs and Hindus in somewhere like Blackburn. Their numbers have crashed because they've been ethnically cleansed – not by us, by the Muslims.

Since Britain is about to overtake Holland as the most over-crowded country in Europe, and over-crowded countries are not comfortable, not healthy, bad for the environment, socially a bad thing, it follows that since mass immigration is causing that, the answer is to stop it. So, yeah, shut the doors. The government spends about £100,000 each year that's available so that ethnic minorities who want to return to their land of ethnic origin can do and be financially helped. There is no moral difference between the Labour Government's £100,000 a year and our £4billion a year. People don't have to go, but a lot would. If people are going to stay, that's fine – we don't have the moral right to throw them out. Our masters invited them in, we sat back and voted for the bastards and didn't bother about it.

A Muslim area here like this will stay like that but they will have to accept that Burnley is an English town, and that England and Britain have certain core cultural traditional philosophical religious values.

It's a matter of accepting and understanding that their religious beliefs and their cultural beliefs and so on have to fit in with ours. If there's a fundamental clash in our society, say in animal welfare where you've got the clash of the instincts of over several hundred years and the tendency overall of the English population.

There's a fundamental clash between that and Halal meat. The Muslims can solve it one of several ways. They either become vegetarians, they eat pre-stunned halal meat and accept Halal meet can be pre-stunned or they leave. It's their choice. But if you have a small but growing population which says that what we want to do is radically unacceptable to the majority of the population then it is utterly unavoidable that there's going to be trouble.

And that is one of the duties of anyone involved in politics – to think long-term and to take unpopular decisions now to avoid worse problems in the future.

In 2005 our manifesto had more words in it than any other party. About ten per cent of it was about immigration and related issues. You can't mention anything about ethnic differences

The liberal media only ever wants to ask me about immigration or Islam and doesn't want to talk about policies we have about globalisation – which are actually far more radical.

Jeremy Clarkson, Jon Gaunt, Richard Littlejohn, it's interesting that most of them are having an impact basically expressing our kind of views but they do so in a way which is just respectable enough to be acceptable. **"**

Yvonne Ridley, 50, journalist. Photographed in London

Ridley was a journalist with the Sunday Express when she made the mistake most reporters dread – she became the story. On September 28, 2001, after being despatched to Pakistan to cover the imminent invasion of Afghanistan in the aftermath of the attack on the Twin Towers, Ridley was captured by the Taliban. She had entered Afghanistan disguised as a Muslim. She was held captive for ten days. Within two years of her release the proud Geordie converted to Islam.

"After 911 I was waiting to go to New York. I was in the airport to get the first flight out but I was told to go to Islamabad. So I hit the ground running with a suitcase full of clothes for New York and nothing for Pakistan. As a journalist you just adapt and after about a week I felt that the best story had to be from ordinary Afghan people so I had to go into Afghanistan. I went full of good intentions into Afghanistan undercover, wearing a burka. Great disguise. Nobody bothered me and then I was caught two days later because a rogue donkey just bolted and went berserk and I fell off.

The truth was I could have got away. As the donkey bolted I'd leaned forward to try and pull it under control. The one piece of equipment I had, a camera, banned under the Taliban, fell out of the folds of my burka right into the passing view of a soldier. And when I hit the ground and stood up he was shouting at me demanding the camera and I took it off and gave it to him and then closed my eyes waiting to be shot. And after 10 seconds, which is a long time when you're waiting to be shot, I opened my eyes and he'd gone. He had gone to find out who hired the donkey, who is in charge of this woman and then he would find out who was responsible for the crime of bringing a camera into the country. And I thought, 'God he didn't realise I'm a Westerner, I can get away'. I joined on to another group and I was still invisible in my magic cloak. I looked behind, I saw my two guides surrounded by a load of angry men with the Taliban soldier. We'd agreed, if things went pear-shaped, it would be every man, or in my case woman, for herself.

I turned round and went back and pushed through the crowd to get to my guides. I was thrown back. In the end I had to take off my burka and shout in a very loud English voice, 'Will somebody let me though!'. You could've heard a pin drop. It was like the parting of the seas and it was, 'where the hell did she come from?' I looked at my guides who I thought were going to overwhelmed by this noble courageous gesture and they looked at me as if to say, 'lady we were in trouble before but now we're in serious trouble'. And we were all arrested and carted off. I was held for ten days. Ten terrifying days and, you know, all the terror was manufactured in my imagination. I was kept in King Charles' Winter Palace in Jalalabad, in a rather comfortable room.

I had the key to my room and the interrogation periods would start with a knock on the door to see if they could get permission to come in or not.

I just thought, well, if they're going to kill me I'm going to go down fighting. So I swore at them, I spat at them, I cursed at them, I went on hunger strike for ten days, I was the prisoner from hell. And they kept telling me, 'you are our guest, you are our sister, you know we want you to be happy'. And I was thinking what the hell is going on here? What don't they understand about evil brutal regime? But it was only when the nightmare ended after those ten days I realised that they were, to me at least, courteous and respectful. Which is why I think thank God I was captured by the most evil brutal regime in the world and not by the Americans. For the first six days I was in Jalalabad and was horrible to all of them.

The last four days I was moved to this horrendous jail in Kabul and was even worse in my behaviour.

On the sixth day in Jalalabad this religious cleric came to see me and when I saw him I thought, well this is it, you know, Goodnight Vienna, when the clerics are involved I'm done for. But in fact he said to me, 'Would you like to convert to Islam?' And I thought if I say 'yes' he'll say you're an insincere fickle woman take her away and have her stoned. If I say 'no' I'll be accused of insulting Islam and I'll be taken away and stoned. So in the end I said, 'look, I can't make such a life-changing decision but if you let me go when I get back to London I promise I will read the Koran'.

I still went to church, to St James' Church in Piccadilly. I went there twice a month, which in some people's eyes in Britain is bordering on fanaticism. But I found the Koran very easy because all the people who are in the Bible are in the Koran with the exception of the Prophet Muhammad.

I think what people found difficult was the big leap that I made, the dramatic change in my lifestyle. I was a Bigg Market girl, I was a party girl. I worked hard and I played hard and led a very a hedonistic lifestyle. A very pleasure-seeking lifestyle. I wasn't a bad person, but my life was drifting, it was pretty meaningless, but in Islam I stopped drinking, eventually stopped smoking, stopped dating or any sort of casual relationships, and my mum and dad were delighted – until I actually converted and they were even more in shock when I put on the hijab.

People now, when they see me, they see a hijab they see a Muslim woman. And you can see all the word association flashing through their minds: Bin Laden, terrorism, and then Yvonne Ridley – Taliban supporter, simply because I told the truth about my treatment.

The press have a great deal of responsibility, a huge responsibility to blame for whipping up the Islamophobia. We are judged on our faith as Muslims. You never read about a Christian burglar or a Jewish burglar or a Hindu burglar or a Sikh bank robber but, my God, if anyone does anything bad and they're a Muslim, Muslim is immediately in the headline.

Everybody was trying to second guess what I would say [when I was released]. And in fact I'm told one headline writer had put 'Rapist' in the headlines. So they were furious when I came out and said I was treated with respect and courtesy. It's like, 'no, no, no, we don't want to hear that. We want to hear about the rape, the buggery, the sodomy, the burns, the torture, the brutality', in fact what later materialised in Abu Ghraib.

My daughter said to me a couple of years ago, 'I just want a normal mother'. I said, 'what do you mean a normal mother?' She said 'one who hasn't been captured by the Taliban. It's so embarrassing'.

That was the whole focus. Everybody forgot I was a journalist. Nobody minds John Simpson or Rageh Omar or any of the men going into the war zone even though they have families and children. But I came under this outrageous focus as a mother. And I thought, hang on, what happened to equality?

I ended up being targeted by a group of women columnists whose views could have come from the Taliban."

David Quincey, 45, homeless. Photographed in Crawley

Since being forced to return to Britain following his deportation from Thailand in 2004, Quincey has been homeless. For much of that time he has lived in Gatwick and Heathrow airports.

 I've been homeless since I came back from Thailand. My Thai wife paid somebody to push me off a third-story balcony. While I was in a coma in intensive care she emptied my bank account of £75,000. I landed back in Gatwick with £23 in my pocket. I had nowhere to go, I've got no family in this country. I went into the airport coffee shop and started chatting away to a few guys and they were living there. They showed me where to sleep and what to do. I hadn't a bag with me, it was the middle of winter.

I left the air force in 1986 after seven and a half years. I had basically retired over there. Semi-retired. I built a house, had a couple of cars. That was three years ago.

I spent three months in a coma. I died three times. I had a tracheotomy, my spleen was removed, drains in both lungs, drains in my pancreas. That's why I've got this stick now. My neck and my back is no good. I was in hospital for five months in total. I had a visit from the British Embassy and they said, 'the minute you leave this hospital you're going to get arrested because you are on overstay on your visa'. I said, 'excuse me, I've been in a coma for three months, how am I supposed to leave the country?'. I discharged myself from the hospital – I just walked out, didn't tell anybody. I just said I was going for a cigarette. I went to the north to see if I could get my money and I did get arrested. I went from one jail in the north to another, then I went to the Bangkok Hilton, stayed in there for a while. I was in jail in total for about seven months. I was just waiting for them to deport me.

At the Bangkok Hilton you've got a room and you lay on the floor with a blanket. It is literally jam-packed with people. The room is about ten feet by six feet.

The only thing you get is rice. They do it in big pots. In the morning they bring you rice and fish-head stew or chicken bones and stew. You can see all the rats and cats jumping into these pots through the bars. Then they bring you rice again for lunch. Obviously you've got to wash it because you've seen what's happened to the pots. You get the fish-head stew again with chilli in it. And at night time you get fish-head stew with rice again but it's got more chilli in

it. That's what you survive on. That's it, that's all you get. I still had my bags in as well, all my drains. I was at rock bottom. I couldn't move my left arm at all. I literally had to sit with my arm and just move it 500 hundred times a day. I couldn't move my fingers. I damaged my neck and my back but the only thing I broke was my collarbone. That was from hitting the ground.

I was in Gatwick. Then I moved to Heathrow. Because I have no bag and passport or anything, when the police came round I would say, 'I'm waiting for a flight, waiting for the ticket desk to open'. Once they get to know your face they know exactly what you're doing. They say you've got to leave the airport. So all you used to do is walk down the stairs. And they'd walk off and you would come back up the stairs and just go to a different place and go back to sleep again and hope you didn't get woken up the next time. They were never nasty. The staff at the airports are very good. They know who is living there. They'll give you free food when they're closing their shops. There was about 20 of us.

I went to the council and I said to them, 'look, this is my situation', and the funny thing was all over the walls was if you're an asylum seeker we'll do this for you we'll do that for you. And the guy said to me, 'there's nothing we can do'. I said, 'can't you put me in a B&B? I'm homeless'. I still had one bag at this stage – straight in my pancreas. It should have been attended to but obviously it wasn't. I ended up going to the hospital and I was in there for about a month, they cleared everything up for me and made sure I was okay.

I came to Crawley to come to Crawley Open House. The worst thing about being on the streets is that you've got absolutely nothing to do except drink. So when I'm on the streets all I'm doing is drinking, drinking, drinking. And I've come in here and basically de-toxed myself. I mean it's absolutely fantastic, the way this place works is so different to any other hostel that I've been in.

The hostels, they're basically locked in an office. Whereas here you have got people like Malcolm who will help with drink and all of these sorts of things. They think I have got post-traumatic stress disorder from my

fall because I still get very bad flashbacks and nightmares. With the injuries to my back I'm taking about 30 tablets a day, painkillers, muscle relaxants.

If you can imagine I've come from a lifestyle where basically I was living like a king to sleeping on the floor in Gatwick and begging in Hounslow. Living on the streets is very demoralising. Okay, I drink when I'm on the streets and I drink a lot because you are very depressed. People just treat you as if you look like shit. People don't want you there, or want to know who you are and what you're doing.

I've seen people deliberately overdose on drugs, I've seen people kill themselves because they've got so far down. It's rough and a lot of people don't understand that it can happen to anybody at any age. I never thought it would happen to me. Not for one minute did I think it could happen to me. Ever. I've seen people who have been exceptionally well off. Then there's been arguments with their wives, lost everything and ended up on the streets.

There is a community spirit at the airport, [but it's] a bit different to on the streets. When people start anything there's always someone who will stop them because they will get us all into trouble. I've seen people knocked out deliberately just so they'll go to sleep. A guy's just gone and punched him. For his own good and for everybody else's good. In the morning they've woke up and can't remember a thing.

[At the airport] everything is shared out between us all. Sometimes it does get a bit frightening. When we were going to sleep everybody would split up. And generally we would go to sleep in twos, but apart. So if anything was happening you've always got each other to look after each other. We'd be a decent distance apart but within eye range.

You can just get washed in the toilets. Again, you'll get people who'll give you aftershaves. They've just come off the aeroplane, they're still in the holiday mood. If we got a carton of cigarettes they would all be shared out. I'd say it is a community spirit.

If it wasn't for places like this, if I had have stayed out on the streets, because I haven't got a spleen, I'm very susceptible to colds and all that sort of thing, by now I would have had hypothermia.

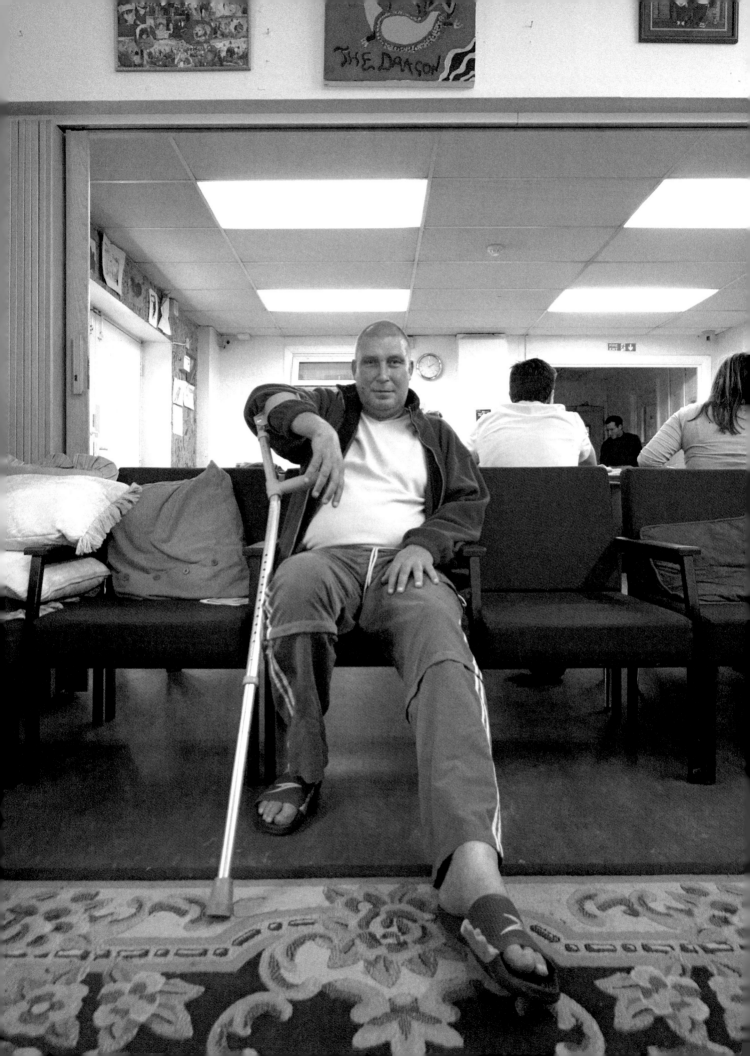

Sean Carr, 39, lead singer, Death Valley Screamers. Photographed in Kiev, Ukraine

Carr was working on Leeds' Kirkgate Market as a cobbler when he decided to move to Ukraine after meeting and marrying Zhenya, the daughter of Ukraine Prime Minister Yuliya Tymoshenko. He invited friend Mick Lake to join him with the intention of re-recording the music they had written together as teenagers. Their traditional rock sound was an instant success and Death Valley Screamers were soon playing their 20-year-old songs in front of 250,000 people at the Independence Day concert in Kiev.

I had a cobblers business. Mick was in music, dance music type of thing. We kept in touch with each other and we started rehearsing together after my dad died. I had a cottage to myself in the middle of nowhere so we had the opportunity to rehearse. Nobody for miles around.

And that's basically how it started. I met Jen and I came over here. I brought all my stuff over with me and I just happened to have our first cassette, demo cassette. And I said, 'listen to this'. And I thought my God what have I done. She listened to it and she said, 'you've got to do this, you've got to start playing music over here'.

I met these three guys. They were in a cover-versions band and I just said to them, 'do you fancy doing real rock and roll, our own type of stuff?' They said yeah. So basically when I moved over here I had some spare money that I'd brought with me. Jen was out doing her thing and I didn't know anybody at the time. So I rang Mick up and said, 'I've met these three guys, how would you fancy reprising the album that we never got round to recording?'.

It was first made when I was 17, in the late eighties. We played anything from the Duchess of York in Leeds to Dingwalls in London, right through the University scope. We had EMI interested right at the last point. The band was called Paris In The Fall. But one thing led to another and we all split up and went our separate ways.

I said let's just do it. Take a month, rehearse and do it, have some fun, we've got something to remember us by. Next thing we know the record company got hold of it. The rest, as they say, is history.

One minute I'm working in Leeds market doing my own thing, the next thing I've got loads of press in my face. So, honestly, yeah, it's a big, big step. Not one I was prepared for. It's been a rollercoaster. Scary at times. Just facing the world press for example. Imagine you being you then all of a sudden the next day you walk out and you've got half of the world's press in your face. It's daunting. It's scary.

We played to 250,000 people. Pretty nerve-wracking. It was televised to 60 million people. At the time we didn't know that. It's been hard work, obviously with my mother-in-law and

being who my mother-in-law is and the band. We got a lot of flak saying, 'oh, he's riding on the back of his mother-in-law'. But now we've sort of like done it off our backs. Stood up and been proud and we've had three No.1s here and played to God knows how many thousands of people.

And the press are now seeing us for what we are rather than what they thought we were. For some reason they seem to like us. Whether it's because we're colourful characters or that we do something a bit different from the normal over here. We're the only guys doing this. They have been supportive. And in all fairness they've not written one bad word about us. You get a lot saying, 'can we interview you and the band?', and then at the end of the interview they say, 'can we ask you some questions about your mother-in-law?' You just think piss off – go and ask her, not me. Alright, we've established that it's not an ordinary situation, it's an extraordinary situation. If we were a normal rock and roll band if you like, we're nothing special, but we don't actually ring the press up and say, 'would you like to interview us?'. They're interested in what we're doing.

I was sat at home with my daughter last year. And we went on to DVS's website and she said, 'can I write something on your website?'. And I said, 'of course you can, yeah'. She wrote, can't remember the exact words, but she said, 'thank you very much for looking after my dad even though he's getting old and can't really sing, only joking dad, love you really'. We were sat in Leeds. Within seconds some girl from Christ-knows-where turned round and said, 'dear Charlotte, you ought to be very, very proud of your father and his band for what he's done and achieved in Ukraine. You should be very, very proud. We all love him'. And that came back within seconds. And that kind of meant a lot.

We've had several hits. We've hit the charts in Russia, Egypt, Israel, Moldova, obviously here in Ukraine. We were supposed to play in England last year at some charity do's and the British Government wouldn't give our three Ukrainian's visas. They said they weren't going to come home. What a load of bullshit. At the time we were No.1 – you know who we are, you know what we do, you know we want

to go and play. They made it as hard as possible. I said we want to go and do some charity gigs. They said you need a work permit, but I said we weren't working. They said you're still working technically. It was a farce, load of bullshit. Consequently they stamped 'Denied' on all three of their passports which give us the kiss of death for Europe. So we can't play outside Ukraine at the minute.

We don't make a penny. We do gigs and get £80. You don't get extra when they show your videos over here or anything like that. You have to pay 600 dollars every time they show the damn thing on the television.

Record sales, they pay you a price up front and then that's it, done. Then afterwards the distribution company, if you get paid for 2000 CD's you get, like, a less than a dollar per CD. They get sold for two and half quid, five dollars. Then we ring the record company up about our sales and they say, 'well, we've got no records of what's going on'. So you never know if there's thousands that have gone out or not.

Jen, my wife, not many 27-year-old women would say, 'go and do it, go and kick some ass'. That's the best thing. Probably the main reason why I want to stay here because obviously she's supporting her mum. If there was none of that then I would insist strongly on leaving. I speak fluent French and fluent Spanish. I pick languages up like that. This one, it's absolutely hard picking it up.

Everything is backwards from what we've been taught over there. You can go down the road you've got bicycles coming at you. You've got locks, they are upside down. You've got locks on the outside of toilets.

If I said it was easy I'd be a liar. I've got a beautiful daughter over in England. I miss all my friends. There's not a week goes by where I don't have a little cry to myself or see something of Yorkshire.

You sit and watch a bit of telly and see Last of the Summer Wine for example and I'll have a little cry to myself. Silly things that you never even watched in England and you sit and watch it on Sky and you say, 'God, that's my home, that's where I'm from'.

Yorkshire is an absolutely beautiful place.

Jack Hughes, 83, war veteran. Photographed in Preston

In 1943, at the age of 18, Hughes joined the Royal Navy as a quarter gunner, defending ship convoys around the globe during the Second World War. He married in 1949 and had three children.

 We went for the medical and I said, 'what am I going into?'. And they said, 'we're recruiting for the Royal Navy'. We went to Pontins Holiday Camp in Pwllheli. HMS Glendower. Did our seven weeks seamanship course and then went and did a full week gunnery course. And then they said, 'we're going to draft you'. We had to go to Greenock in Scotland, on the Clyde, to pick our ship up – HMS Stalker.

We were what they called an escort carrier and we used to escort convoys. There was Stalker, Hunter and Attacker. They were converted American banana boats. Originally we got ten of them. I can't name them all – Hunter, Stalker, Attacker, Khedive, Striker, Trumpeter. I forget the others. They were on the lease and they had to be returned after the war.

It was New Year's Day when we went on it, 1944. We did a convoy to Gibraltar, then went on to Malta. Then we came back to the UK, picked up another convoy and did the same. And then we went down to Crete and Greece.

We left the Mediterranean in January 1944 and went out to the Far East. I was in the Far East from then until we came home in 1945.

The most problem time was dawn and dusk, when the submarines used to strike because we couldn't see them, the planes couldn't go out. Once or twice I've been on the boat's deck and Boom! Just on dawn a submarine has torpedoed and hit one of the supply ships. That's the most vulnerable time.

We was out at sea and all of a sudden we heard these shells coming over [whistles] and we thought: Japanese! And it wasn't, it was our big battle ship HMS Howe and she was firing shells ashore and they were passing over the top of us. We could hear the whistles. The first one was scary and then when we looked out at sea and there was just a speck on the horizon – HMS Howe. These 16inch guns, they could fire a long way.

I was on a four-inch gun. Our planes sunk about six submarines, flying round you could spot them. They carried either one 500lb bomb, or two 250lb bombs. And they dropped them on the submarines. But we didn't know until the pilots landed back on and gave a report to the flight officer. And then it was tannoyed all through the ship, you see. We cheered, a big cheer went up.

The four-inch guns. We had Oerlikon, they called them pom-poms and then they had the smaller gun – Bofors. Two Bofors on the starboard side and two Bofors on the port side.

I was a quarter gunner. I fired it a lot. I think we got one Japanese ship. We couldn't see them. They were out of sight. The Gunnery Officer, he can direct you which way to elevate you or manoeuvre it round.

Nervous? No not really. Right at the beginning I was, yes, what you're going into, but you got used to it, took it in your stride.

You had three watches: Red, white and blue. Each one took over from the other and each one did four hours watching. We used to bed down on the deck, there was always one awake.

You got used to it in the end, oh aye, we're bigger than you, we can shoot you before you shoot us.

If the Japanese planes came over you always had to watch for the one who didn't do any dogfighting – and he was the Kamikaze pilot. Next minute he aims himself at whatever target he wants. There could be 50 merchant ships and three carriers plus destroyers. Cruisers, destroyers and carriers, we had the job to protect the convoy. But you always had to look for one who didn't do anything.

They nearly always got shot down because there was 20 or 30 navy ships firing at it. Bound to hit it. Three suicide planes tried to hit us but they got shot down.

When we were on Rangoon we had to go ashore guarding the ammunition on the airfield. There were two planes there, two Japanese planes and one was a Kamikaze plane. Zeroes – called Zeroes. And there was a band in it and once that pilot got in it he was strapped in and couldn't get out. You had to die. You had to die, there was no turning back. He daren't go back to his airfield or anything like that, he would have to blow himself up. Because that's their religion, die for the flag. For their country. They never returned home. And they never hit anything.

We had no radio, no news. It was only when the Americans dropped two atom bombs on Hiroshima and Nagasaki, when that went on, the Japanese surrendered. And that came over the microphone: The war is now ended. Hooray! Big shouts.

I came home on the 29 July, 1945. I was an apprentice at Leyland Motors, used to work in a sawmill for the Leyland buses, fire engines and ambulances.

There should never be any wars. Somebody has got to suffer in a war. And it's always one man who wants to do it: Mussolini, Hitler, Japanese the same – Emperor Hirohito. There's only people get killed and suffer and that. I disagree with wars. But mind you, I won't be a conscientious objector and not go in the forces. If you've got to go in, well, I'll go in.

I have respect for the armed forces, but I've no time for the United Nations because after the war Russia, England, America, French joined with the idea of if any problems came up now they would send, not to fight, but they would send thousands of servicemen as strength, power. Instead of us doing it, the Americans are doing it on their own – that's what the United Nations were for. And you could call on them to provide a mixed armed force to go to any problem throughout the world and just force, not fight. They knew that if all these countries were against them, there wouldn't be any fighting. It never happened.

I think the government supports war veterans, but the government doesn't do as well as the British Legion. Oh they should do, aye, they should do. But with the British Legion nobody is turned away. Anybody genuine calls, they get support, no question. I used to go round, welfare officer, take the details.

I'm well off, to tell the truth. Like this sheltered accommodation. They've just done that kitchen, ripped it all off, a new kitchen. My heating, I have to pay for my heating but me being upstairs you get all the heat from downstairs and I never switch my heating on. Even in winter. I get Attendance Allowance which is £60 a week. I get pension grants which is bugger all. I fought for it. I'm living the life of luxury.

I have to give a little speech at Armistice Sunday. The Kohima Epitaph: 'When you go home tell them of us and say, for your tomorrow, we gave our today'. I say it every year.

Daniel Twiddy, 27, Iraq War veteran. Photographed in Stamford

On March 25, 2003, L/Cpl Twiddy was sleeping on top of his Challenger 2 tank on the banks of the Shatt-al-Basra canal in Basra, Iraq, when another British unit – Black Watch – mistakenly launched an attack on his unit. Two of Twiddy's fellow Queen's Royal Lancers were killed – Corporal Stephen Allbutt, 35, and Trooper David Clarke, 19. Twiddy was blown off the tank and sustained severe injuries. He has subsequently had extensive skin grafts and surgery to his face and body. He now owns a plastering business in Stamford, Lincolnshire.

I joined army straight from school. I was with the Queens Royal Lancers, Royal Armoured Core – tank regiment. I served with them for six years. I served in Bosnia, Kosovo, Cyprus on operational tours.

This was my first time in Iraq. We were there waiting in Kuwait until they declared war so we were the first ones there.

I never had desert boots. Some of us were in green combats and normal black combat boots which weren't made for the desert, so the heat melted the glue in them, the sand got in them and basically ripped them apart. It's the Ministry of Defence – goes down to money, lack of money, shortage of kit and things which they say never happened but did. I was there in my desert boots. They were falling apart. My commander died in green combats. It's a statement that he died in green kit and not desert kit.

We had to take over some bridges on a canal on the outskirts of Basra. If we saw any enemy we could ask permission to take them out. On bridge four, was the 2 RTR Royal Tank Regiment, part of the Black Watch battle group. We found a small crossing, a dam line between our bridge and the bridge on our right. They thought that it was being used for supplies, people crossing, Iraqi troop movements.

At night we started up a routine between the two tanks so people could sleep. I just finished my part at about 1am. I woke up my tank commander, he got into the tank and started looking through the night sights, patrolling the area and that. I went to get to sleep. The driver was asleep in his driving position, the gunner was on top of the tank. I was on top of the tank. It was quite warm out there with the tank being warm. It's cramped in the tank. There was no immediate threat. At about half-one I got woken with a massive explosion, blowing me off the tank. I was still awake at this point. I could hear screaming and shouting. I thought it was the enemy. I could hear my commander shouting at me, 'roll yourself out'. I managed to roll myself away. The distance was about six or seven metres I got blown off the tank. Even to fall off the tank it's a fair distance. Also the gunner got blown off. I could

hear him screaming, I was on fire but I couldn't see much, the flash had burned my eyes. The explosion did my hearing in. It was chaos.

They must have fired again. The first one that came in didn't cause damage to us because it missed us. But it was still powerful enough to cause us a lot of damage. The people inside the tank were still alive. The second round they fired hit our tank spot on – you couldn't ask for a better shot really. It killed our commander instantly and the driver instantly. It was said that it was such a good shot that it passed right through the commander.

That explosion threw a lot on top of us again, set me on fire again. I managed to roll myself off again. I can remember being on my hands and knees. I couldn't see because blood was coming down my face. I just thought I'm going to die, this is it. I'm just going to roll over and go to sleep. As I rolled over and went to sleep I started thinking about home and things, then someone came over to me and says, 'Twiddy, Twiddy you're going to be alright'. In the background I heard machine guns. I heard the tractor ambulance which is a noise you would never forget. I remember them putting me in the back, seeing a few faces and then they must have injected me with morphine. I woke up nearly two weeks later in a hospital in England.

I didn't feel pain. They didn't think I was going to live. The body did its job, the adrenaline kicks in. The doctors said the burns actually burned through the nerves' supply system so you don't feel that anyway.

Altogether I've had 25 or so operations. I had 80 per cent burns to my head and hands, they were all skin grafted. Then I had large cuts and bruising to my head. That was stapled together. Also I had a large piece of shrapnel going through the left-hand side of my face. It went straight through my face, my cheekbone, jawbone. So I had a chunk of flesh taken out of my side and put into there.

Also had a lot of metalwork put into my face to reconstruct my cheekbone. I lost my hearing totally in my left ear. That's non-recoverable. My right ear was damaged through tone damage – I can't hear high frequency notes. My eyes they managed to save, they were badly burned and they had shrapnel in them. They managed to save both of them. Shrapnel

wounds to my face and also burns to my face. I got brought back to England to Broomfield Hospital in Chelmsford, which is one of the country's best burns unit. They have been really good there, I couldn't have asked for better treatment. It's an NHS hospital.

Once I came home I couldn't do anything for myself. I still had my jaw wired up so I couldn't even open my mouth and eat. I had to eat everything through a straw.

People had to be off work to make sure I was eating. All this was non-recoverable from the MOD. And changing my dressing twice a day and also to be there to apply creams to all my skin grafts just to make sure they were supple. So I approached a civilian company where I live in Stamford, they would do it for £60 a week and the MOD refused to pay that.

I felt let down totally. I feel they've been bad the way they've treated me. I've had no compensation through this whatsoever. It's just the fact that they won't admit liability. They still deny that they were in the wrong – even though it was friendly forces, from the British forces. We've had no apology from them.

The MOD just think once you're signed off and discharged that's it, they're finished with you. They've caused this to happen to me and it's going to be with me for the rest of my life. And they should be there for the rest of my life helping me and dealing with it.

It's not just the physical side it's the mental side as well. That's what affects people. I did need to talk about things and I went to see someone at the military. They were three hours away. They went through a few questions and said, 'well, if there's anything else we can do for you, you've got our number'. That was it.

I have the occasional nightmares, but nothing like I used to at the start – terrible ones.

There should be safety devices put on to vehicles and given to the soldiers when they are fighting so no friendly fires can happen, such as a Blue Force Tracker which the Americans have, a device which they carry so as soon as you lock on to a person or a vehicle it tells you they are a friendly force.

The Ministry of Defence won't provide that because of the cost. Obviously life is less important than the cost of a piece of equipment.

Ian, 42, protestor. Photographed on Parliament Square, London

From 2001 until his death in 2011, Brian Haw lived in a tent near the Houses of Parliament to protest against war, most notably Britain's involvement in the invasion of Iraq and Afghanistan. Despite various court actions, Haw was granted legal permission to protest on Parliament Square in 2006. Early in 2007 Ian, who does not belong to any political group, began camping alongside Haw. Ian, who likes to be known as 'Friend', has no legal right to camp on Parliament Square.

"Technically, according to birth certificates and things like that, I am 42 years old. But at the same time I am the same age as you and the same age as all the matter in the universe. We are all of the same type and the same star.

I have been here simultaneously far too long and not long enough. I am trying to change the consciousness of the human race. As far as I'm aware, we're a parasitic life form that is devoiding our host planet of the ability to support life and I need to be part of a symbiotic life form that is supporting all the life on its own planet. To me, this is a mental health issue.

I've been on the pavement here for about a month and a half, but I'm not very good at time. I only found out it was Friday today. Camping out is a strange phrase. Most people think camping is something you do as a holiday. I've been sleeping in God's tent here on a regular basis for that period of time. But it's not really camping. This is my duty to serve, my duty to care. And I'm trying to do my duty to care for all of creation, all of life.

The fossil fuels that we use generated health and vitality in the atmosphere when they were living. As we dig them up and redefine them in the atmosphere we take away its health and vitality. At the moment, the way that we're working, the way that we're living, it's irreplaceable. You grow a crop such as hemp – hemp would be the most beneficial crop we could grow and we should be growing lots of it. It fixes carbon from the atmosphere, in a very abundant way. We can use its fibre for making paper, we can make clothes out of it, we can make very good materials out of it. In fact we can make almost anything that we want out of hemp. It produces seeds which we can use as food. It produces omega 3 oils and such that we can use for our health and vitality. The amount of medicinal uses of hemp are phenomenal, I can't list them. It's a little bit beyond where I'm at. I'm no good at retaining information.

Do I smoke hemp? I like to smoke pot, yes. And I don't see anything wrong with it. It helps me stay mellow, stay chilled. I find it stops my joints from aching so much. It actually benefits me in other ways. I would like it if there was enough hemp in the world for me to eat it rather than smoke it. Because eating hemp is actually very beneficial for us. Because it has got anti-carcinogens and all sorts of other bits and pieces that benefits our beings rather than detracting from our beings.

I believe that every individual has got to be able to stand up and represent themselves. I'm trying to push for democracy which is you vote for you and I vote for me. If we vote for somebody to represent us the only person they are going to represent is themselves. And therefore we've got to learn to represent ourselves. And in a true democracy, if we should ever have one, we all represent ourselves, every single individual and there's not an age limit. Small children have got every bit as much of a right to say what they think as anybody else. You could say that they don't know as much but, let's face it, how much do adults know? Education, education, education. Power is knowledge and controlled power is controlled knowledge. In order to have a police force you've got to have crime. In order to have a police force that is large enough to protect the government you've got to have a lot of crime. Which is why drugs are illegal. It perpetuates a lot of crime.

I sleep in this tent which is God's tent. One man has been here for seven years and he's been campaigning to try and get the troops out of Afghanistan and Iraq. I think that is just a single facet of a very big problem. There's pollution, there's environmental degradation.

I live upon Planet Hope and I don't consider any part of it more my home or less my home than any other part of it.

I haven't earned money for 12 years. I gave it up, knocked it on the head. As soon as I became aware that we're destroying our own future, our own environment, and all the life on this planet for money, I became sick of it and actually gave it up. I walked out of the tax office I told them that I wasn't willing to earn money anymore, I wasn't willing to take part in it and that was it. They asked me if I could write a letter, I asked them for help with my spelling. I drafted a letter on the counter and handed it in. They've taken me at my word and I've acted on my word.

I've gone pretty much on trust. Sometimes I've been helped. I've got friends who have refitted me clothes-wise. I've had girlfriends, re-painted people's houses and they have fed me. But I haven't done it for that. In order for me to be able to do it, I need energy putting in. So people have put the energy in.

My mother and father believe in democracy. They believe the government is doing the right thing for them, and they believe that the police force has never lied. They believe all sorts of strange things that I can't go along with. They believe that smoking pot will give me mental health problems, because they've been told that. They've been educated to believe that. Whereas I think that people that have got mental health problems may turn to using pot. The truth and the unreality that gets told is quite strange. An awful lot of people that don't feel they fit in and such like will turn to drugs because they don't feel they fit in. It's very difficult to fit in to a society that is destroying itself, that is destroying its own future.

I am here in the middle of London to be as annoying as I possibly can so that the many-headed beast of the apocalypse can swallow me and I can choke the fucker. And as to what that's all about I don't even know. But that's the mission. The mission is to try and choke the beast of the apocalypse and get on with having a future. If I can't see a positive change in the way that we're living within three years then I think we're going to leave. I'm here illegally. I don't have a licence to be here. I don't have any certification to say I'm allowed to be here. I haven't applied, I'm not going to apply. And I'm breaking the law by my presence here – I'm a criminal, by presence, being here trying to change the way that we live.

I would like to be able to smoke pot 24/7, well not 24/7 but four or five joints a day. Being here, well, if I have any pot, if I find some, if I come across some, if anybody gives me some, the chances are the police will take it off me fairly shortly after I get it.

I would not have children without the ability to know that they had a future. Because if they haven't got a future bringing them into the shit world doesn't seem like a viable thing to do. In fact it seems like quite a ghastly thing to do.

So I need to change the future in order to even conceive having a child.

Queen's Guard, age unknown. Photographed at St James's Palace, London

The distinctive bearskin-wearing Queen's Guard are permanently stationed outside Buckingham Palace and St James's Palace. The foot soldiers are from five regiments: the Grenadier Guards, Coldstream Guards, Scots Guards, Irish Guards and Welsh Guards. They have guarded the Sovereign Palaces since the 17th Century. They are not allowed to speak while on duty.

Sarah Batten, 36, suffers from cerebral palsy. Photographed in Bristol

Despite suffering from an incredibly isolating condition, Sarah leads an active life. Through the Outsiders dating agency she is hoping to find a partner to fulfil her sexual needs.

" Cerebral Palsy occurs when the brain is starved of oxygen during birth, so part of the brain dies. CP means the body doesn't receive messages from the brain properly, hence jerky movements and speech problems. My brain will tell my right hand to pick a pen up. Instead of just picking the pen up my arm and hand will be jerky, possibly knocking the pen away; my fingers and thumb might not close round the pen at the right time. Finally I will pick the pen up.

I live in a flat in Thornbury, a small town just outside Bristol. I live here on my own.

Cerebral Palsy isn't an illness it's a disability, like blindness and deafness. For me CP is isolating. First I have the barrier of the wheelchair and then there's the barrier of my speech.

With people who are used to my speech I talk normally, with people who aren't I use a Lightwriter. I don't get frustrated because I'm used to it. If someone is bothering to try to understand me, then it's up to me to stay calm.

It varies how people treat me, depending on how well they know me. I do find the more people are around me the better they get; until they realise I'm the same as anyone else – I just need a hand with things. E-mails are much more fluent, whereas face-to-face conversation is slower. I guess when people meet me their preconceptions come into play. Also, I'm really shy with people I don't know, which doesn't help matters.

It's very, very difficult finding a partner mainly due to people's preconceived ideas about disabled people and adult relationships. Also my speech impairment causes problems in the initial stages. Thirdly, getting to meet the right kind of people is extremely difficult.

I have had limited experience at conducting relationships since living at the flat. However, the plus side to not having carers all the time is that I could have time alone with someone. Not needing carers to put me to bed would be a huge advantage if having a relationship. For this reason I want someone more able than me, otherwise I don't think it would work for me.

The difficulty for me would be going places together. If he was disabled I would need a carer to come with me. If he was able-bodied he would have to assist me in and out of the car and lift my chair in and out of the car, I would also need him to feed me. These things could well pose another barrier.

E-mails are great for starting relationships, but in my experience getting to next stage is the difficult part. E-mails are fluent and you can get to know someone quite well. However there comes a point when you move to the next stage or the e-mails just fizzle out.

In my experience people think that people with CP or other disabilities are not capable physically, mentally or emotionally of having adult relationships. Therefore people think we don't know about sex, and what's more, we shouldn't know about sex. It makes me laugh how some people who accept that I've got two A-Levels still can't accept that I know about sex.

When some people have realised that I am fully sexually aware, they have found it hilariously funny for some reason. Probably because they are just not expecting it, which is really sad. People are scared to acknowledge disabled people as sexual beings because it would make things difficult for them.

At school I had boyfriends and since living at the flat I have had one sexual relationship and a one night stand. Some of the people that I socialise with do take the time and trouble to wait for me to use the Lightwriter and actively include me and some of them don't really bother with me. I do appreciate the people that make the effort with me and as far as people who don't, my reaction is if they can't be bothered then neither can I. It doesn't offend or upset me, it's usually people I'm not keen on anyway!

The hardest period in my life was when I moved in to the flat and met the love of my life. I also met for the first time, through him, all the preconceptions able-bodied people have about disabled people and sex.

I didn't have any private carers or Lightwriter back then, so I was really isolated and devastated at that point.

I am a member of Outsiders. I think the concept of Outsiders is great. Getting people in similar circumstances in touch by letter, e-mail and/or by phone.

Also having lunches in various parts of the country for people to meet up, is such a good and safe way of meeting people.

Outsiders also campaigns to make people aware that disabled people can and do have adult feelings and relationships.

I have e-mailed some guys from Outsiders; but as I said before e-mails tend to fizzle out after a while; I haven't got to the next stage with anyone yet. I do enjoy going to the West Country lunches, they're a good crowd.

I, personally, think people see disabled as being child-like people, so to acknowledge disabled people as sexual beings would be unacceptable.

I also think for some it's a control thing for people who run residential homes and clubs for disabled people. If they can prevent sexual activity happening in the first place; they won't have to deal with the possible consequences.

"

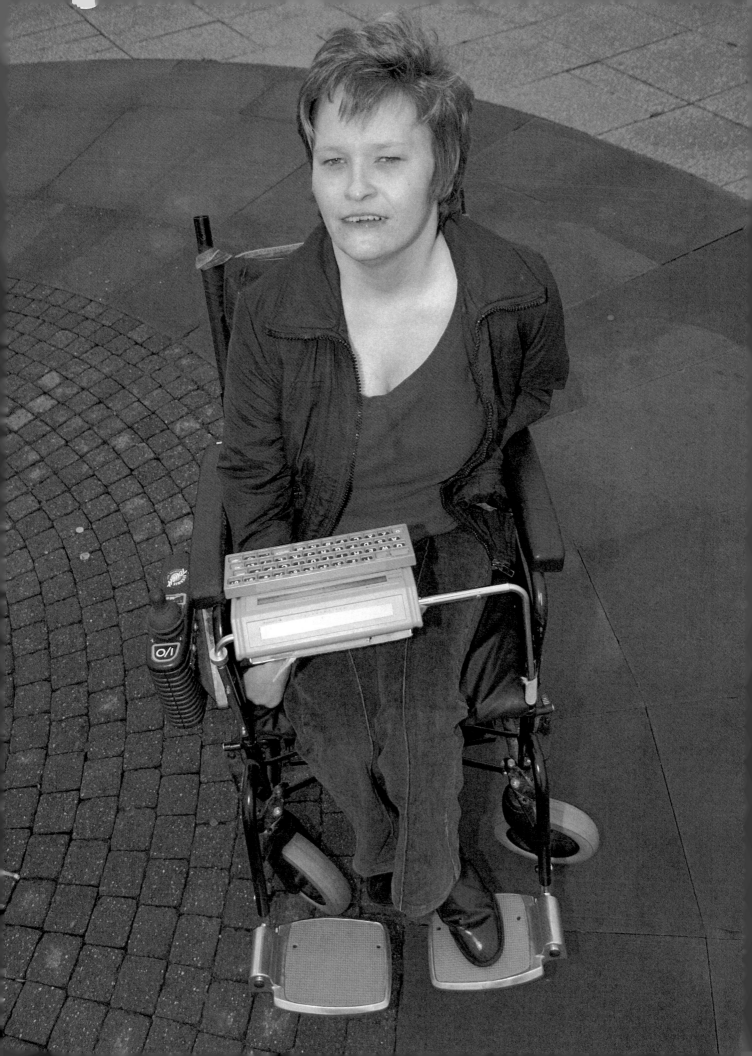

Mistress Sarah Kane, 34, transsexual dominatrix. Photographed in Bury

Since his teens Mark, from Blackpool, has enjoyed cross-dressing. For the past 12 months he has worked as a dominatrix in a small converted house in Bury, Lancashire. Mark, known to his clients as Mistress Sarah Kane, is the only male dominatrix working in the building.

I've been now a dominatrix for ten years. For the last 17 years I've been going out as Sarah on the gay scene. From there I got quite an interest in high heels and the fetish area of things.

We have men who come to see us and most of the men who come to see us are in high-powered kind of jobs. Gasman or a carpet fitter, lawyers. One of my clients who comes to see me actually owns six Vauxhall garages. He comes once every six weeks or so. I've been seeing him for the past three years. He's got a really high-powered job and has a lot of stress. Basically he comes to see me and his main little thing he is into is the caning. He takes severe strokes of the cane. When he leaves here his arse is basically red. He is also into anal play and fisting as well. We have about half a session where we do the anal play a bit which involves inserting stuff into him. And the other half he is being caned.

I have a real passion for wearing shiny latex outfits. And there's a big thing for shiny latex. So people come and see me and we'll put gas masks on and seal ourselves in latex and have general play and fun. There are so many people from different walks of life, each has his kink. I'm also what you call a lifestyle dominatrix who not only does this for a job, I actually do this in my own personal life with a partner.

I actually have a speech impediment which I have had since I was about three or four. It's strange this, when I actually transform myself into Sarah my speech impediment goes. It's an act of confidence. It's like my own confidence changes. I stop being Mark and transform myself into Sarah. Because I'm in complete control, my speech impediment goes away.

You've got to be careful you don't get [your clients] marked. For instance you might have a client who comes to see you who has a wife and girlfriend. They will say to you, 'I want dominating, I want you to tease me'. Lots of them have wives and girlfriends and obviously don't want to be marked. As long as I don't draw blood, fine. As long as you are safe, wear latex gloves for inserting, and condoms.

Before a session we'll always have a consultation, a nice chat and the person will say to me, 'I fancy today being tied up, a bit tied and teased, blindfolded', and basically that

session he'll get teased. Or you will want somebody wanting a corporal punishment session where you use heavy instruments, such as the cane, torture bits and pieces, and you might lay them over the bench and everything, spanked and stuff. Or you get people who are into anal play or water sports. The only thing I don't do is hard sports. Hard sports is basically shit.

We charge either £80 for half an hour or £150 for the hour. We also have people who are in what we call prolonged bondage. They say I want an hour's face time but I want three hours tied up. Every half an hour you go in and see they're alright, have a play with them, leave them in the room in the dark. Occasionally see if they're alright, give them a quick tease.

People will come in and say I want sex with you. We don't offer a sexual service. We're not an escort agency. We can give you a happy ending but what I tend to do is use my cane to make them do it themselves, kind of forced.

People are into fetish. People have a fetish about boots. People have a fetish about foot worship. Heels, latex, PVC. And people just go on the internet and have a look at those things. Some people have a fetish about water sports. Pissed on. Everybody has their own kink. Some are happy just to go on the internet, and just browse it. Pick top-shelf magazines. But then other people want to take it a bit further. They want real-time play. That's when we come in. We offer people real-time play.

There is a lot of people out there into what we call trans-gender, a T-girl. T-girl is a guy who, when dressed, looks like a girl. But the only difference is instead of having a vagina I've got a cock.

I don't see females. The reason I don't see females is I have a girlfriend and we are both bisexual. Basically we have an agreement that I have no problem with my girlfriend going with girls and she has no problem with me going with men. Clearly on opposite ends. But if I was to go with a girl, my girlfriend would just – that would be it. I don't think I've ever been approached by a girl.

The only time I've been approached by girls is when they're in a relationship and they want me to dominate their man. I've had ladies come to a session with their partner. Sit down and

watch. On an average week I probably see two to three clients a day. I work three to four days.

I tend to see clients from twenties to late seventies. Done one [who said], 'can you kidnap me?'. Got this old client where we arranged this stuff. Actually went to this location, the client said, 'I'll be out and about, I'll be wearing such and such an outfit'. So I went there with another mistress, jumped out the car, put a bag over him. Threw him into the boot of the car. Locked the boot. We then drove up to this bit of waste ground, bit of a wood. Dragged him out of the car. Chained him to a tree. Blindfolded him, beat him up and stuff for a while.

We then got back in the car ourselves. He was all tied up. Had a nice brew, bit of coffee. We then untied him, chucked him back in the car and then threw him out on the street.

We have clients who want to come in and they will come in for the whole afternoon and they want to be my own personal maid. They will come into this room. I will help them get dressed into a maid. Put heels on and stockings on and help with the maid outfit.

Basically all day or for the afternoon they will serve me and help serve the other mistresses. Use them as a footstool, use them as a seat, use them as an ash tray. Stick their tongue out and use it as an ash tray. We'll get them to do all the cleaning jobs and if they don't do a job to my satisfaction they will then get punished for it. So you get a guy and I say, 'I want all the windows cleaning'. And if the windows aren't cleaned to my satisfaction they guy is going to get punished. It's as simple as that. The rule in most houses such as this is once you've taken the money off a client and you're in a room locked up you can do what the hell you want.

In some cases, if I get a client I like, yeah, I will do what I want. But that's between us. The main thing with this is the discretion.

To me, you are either born a dom or you're not. You've got to be in that world and actually enjoy it yourself. It's about learning to play with somebody's mind. Learn to play with the mind, body and the soul. Those to me are the three key things. If you crack those three key things over time you will make a good dominatrix.

Megan Phelps, 22, student. Photographed in Topeka, Kansas, United States

Phelps is part of the Westboro Baptist Church whose membership of around 70 people is comprised almost entirely of the Phelps family. The church claims tragic deaths – any death in fact – are God's punishment for America's acceptance of homosexuality. The church has reached a wider audience in recent years through its picketing of US soldiers' funerals holding up banners with slogans like 'Thank God For Dead Soldiers', 'You Are Eating Your Children' and 'God Hates America'. Her favourite sign is 'God Is Your Enemy'.

I wanted to go to law school for a while, actually for a long time since I was little until about six months ago. I have the grades for it and I have the ability but I think that the Lord is coming soon. What I really want to do is be here in this place and do the job that I'm doing now and also find new ways to be of use. Because our whole goal is to publish this message and I want to be a part of that and I want to do everything I can to further that goal.

I help with a lot of the organisational things, planning trips and things. I help reserve cars hotels airline tickets things like that. And then just any of the administrative functions that are required to run this church. I want to be a faithful steward of the gifts God has given me. That means using them to serve God, to preach His message and do my duty to my fellow man to warn them to flee God's wrath, to warn them of the consequences of disobeying God.

What do my fellow students do that I don't? They go out and party, they go out and get drunk, they whore around. We're in the mid-west, the Bible belt where everyone is sort of God-fearing church goers and things like that. That's a big bad lie – they're hypocrites. These girls I go to school with will come in wearing big crosses and out of one side of their mouth talk about how holy they are, how much they love God, how much they love Jesus and stuff and then on the other side of their mouth they are talking about who they whored around with last weekend and who they are going to whore around with next weekend.

They don't serve God in truth. You show that you love God by keeping his commandments and encouraging your fellow man to do the same. So, if I were to say you're not supposed to go out and whore around and then I go out and whore around, I have no moral authority.

They think it's really weird that we don't go out and do the same things that they do. But that's because they don't have the love of the truth, they don't understand the consequences of what they're doing is Hell. What they're doing is living in sin, defying God, living in defiant rebellion. People who see our signs they say, 'oh they're just hateful, oh they're just ignorant'. These are stupid people, unintelligent, uneducated. That's not what we

are. We are intelligent, hard-working people. The problem isn't the messages on the signs or the fact that we're using the signs. The problem is they hate the message itself. The problem is that this message is so unpalatable to the unregenerate man. It's the message itself, not how we go about preaching it. Look at that sign over there. It says, 'Mourn For Your Sins'. They don't mourn for their sins, they're proud of them. They love their sins. So how can you say those words in a way that will not make them so mad that they want to kill you?

How can you say, 'thank God for dead soldiers'? How can you say, 'God hates you', any other way? Because that is what it says, that's what the scriptures say. It says that he hates all workers of inequity. So if you are going to make sin in your vacation, if you are going to dedicate your life to serving yourself, and your lust, God hates you. That is what the Bible says. The standard is you're not supposed to be going round whoring with anybody you can get your hands on.

The consequences of dealing with God are too great to mess around being ambiguous. And that's the example we have in the scriptures.

The Lord Jesus Christ said, 'blessed are you when men hate you and revile you and persecute you for my namesake'. If you have Billy Graham and you've got everyone in the world saying, 'oh, he's a great preacher, he's a great person', you know perfectly well that he is not a servant of God. Because if you're preaching the word of God, it's hated. It's unpalatable to the flesh. Billy Graham is a false prophet.

The love of God, you show that you love your fellow man by warning them of their sins taking them to Hell. You show that you hate them if you don't warn.

You're supposed to search the scriptures daily. And that's where your study and your focus is. We look at everything from the Bible out. So when you see an event like 9/11 or when these kids go to these schools and shoot a bunch of people and kill a bunch of people, when you see all these events fall out day by day you look at it from a scriptural standpoint and you see good to be drawn from 9/11. I said before, this day is a blessing and a curse. A blessing if you obey the Commandments and a

curse if you won't. You're uncomfortable with those signs God Is Your Enemy, because you are ashamed of the word. Because you don't believe it. That's why you'd be ashamed. We go picket a soldier's funeral you think that's wrong. That's because you've got a humanistic mindset. You're looking at it from a human standpoint. Like, 'how would I feel if somebody came with that sign God Is Your Enemy, if I saw that sign at my son's funeral how would that make me feel?'.

That sign is your only hope. So, when you go to those funerals and they say, 'God blessed this family', things like that. Or, 'this dead person is a hero'. Those are lies. God did not bless that family. When you have a child – a lot of these soldiers that are dying are my age and younger – it's not a blessing when your 18-year-old son comes home dead from the battle. Blown up into a million little pieces by an IED built by a dirt-poor Iraqi for less than a cost of a pizza. That is not a blessing, that is a curse. So that's a lie to say that the soldier is a hero. That soldier is fighting for a nation that hates God, that hates his judgements, that has institutionalised sin and rebellion at every level. He's fighting against God – he is not a hero. The only hope for you is to see this message and if God has mercy on you he will soften your heart.

I'm ashamed to be an American. I'm ashamed to be an American because this nation hates God, hates his judgements, is proud and hypocritical and they're in a lot of trouble.

I have no interest in marrying some person who does not want to serve God. Because I know the end of not serving God. I know the consequences. And not only do I know them I preach them. I'm not going to have anything to do with someone who doesn't want to serve God. Who the heck would marry us?

We love anything that gets the message out. And like all these talk shows, these people are filthy perverts. We don't care because the whole point is to get the message out. They think they're making fun of us. All they are doing is helping us.

We do normal things. We just don't do perverted things. They hate us because they hate the message. And that's it. The end. Game over.

Rev Andrew Allington, 51, vicar. Photographed in Stainforth

For the last decade Reverend Allington has been the parish vicar of St Mary's Church in Stainforth, near Doncaster. The former colliery town has a population of around 7,000. In January, 2008, the vicar was attacked in his home by a teenager from the community he works in.

"The doorbell rang at about eight o'clock at night. It was dark outside. I went to the door, opened it, there was a lad there, had his hood up. He said, 'I need your help vicar, can you help me? Can I come in?' I said, 'not really, not this time of night'. He said, 'it's my girlfriend, she's threatening to kill herself'.

So I took a step outside to talk to him and he pushed me with his hands back through the front door and then kicked me in the torso to the ground. I knocked my head against the bottom of the stairs. Then, when I was getting up, he pulled a knife out and he said, 'give me your wallet'. He's come into the hall, shut the front door behind him. Everything went in slow motion a bit. I said, 'I don't keep a wallet' because I keep my money in my back pocket. And then he said, 'well don't try anything', as he waved his knife.

So I gave him the cash in my back pocket which is about 50 pounds. He said, 'go in there', which is the toilet off the hall. I went into the toilet, he shut the door of the toilet behind me and then just scarpered.

It was all over pretty quick. I was obviously shocked at the time, but I thought, that's it, quite exciting. But I didn't realise how shock worked. About two or three days later even a few weeks later I realised I have suffered shock from it. It's not so much fear, it's the adrenaline when you're faced with the situation and then the adrenaline wears off and you start thinking what might have happened. And just the nature of physical assault. I've never been physically assaulted before. It leaves you feeling humiliated. Then there's the anger you feel from that, and dealing with that.

He was in his mid 20s. He's obviously got a drug or alcohol problem and needed cash. There was loads of things he could have taken, laptop computer, mobile phone. But he just wanted cash so, obviously, he could get his fix.

I think I know who it is. I actually know his father. His father comes to our street supper which we run for people with problems.

People have said that it's unbelievable that it should happen to a vicar but it does happen.

Teachers, all professionals, firemen going to put out fires, they are all getting the same agro. But particularly with people with drug and alcohol problems they are not thinking straight, they are only thinking about their next fix. They would do it to their own grandmother at some point. When they are in a desperate situation they sometimes would do anything.

I think many teenagers don't have a connection with the rest of society, that's the problem. In France and the rest of Europe there is a much stronger culture of teenagers and children doing things together with their families. I think this is where the drink problem comes in. That's not happening in Britain. Children are left to do their own thing. And sometimes when the parents are drinking at home they're encouraging their children to drink too much at home as well. The mining communities have a particular strong culture of drinking which, when you are working long hours down the pit, isn't too much of a problem because you are burning it off. But when you are unemployed and you continue in that drinking pattern… we have a significantly lower life expectancy in Stainforth to the communities next door which is about mining and problems with health in this community.

Young people in working-class cultures are picking up this culture of drinking from their parents and then there's the drug problem. Although it's there in middle-class communities, they can afford to cover it up better.

In working-class communities, when you haven't got the finances and the resources to do that, it comes out more in burglaries. And that behaviour affects the whole community.

When I first came, the kids saw me in the garden and they're very bold as brass round here and they asked if I had any jobs to do, like washing the car and things. And very early on some girls said, 'can we cook your tea?', because they saw I was on my own and they assumed that men can't cook. I agreed to it and then quickly realised that I was going to have to set some boundaries around that. So basically they can book in on a Monday or a Thursday tea time. They have to have a parental consent form and we always have a lady from church come to help me and is present. There is always two adults present.

Over the last six or seven years we've had over 160 children from the age of four to the age of 16 come in, three or four at a time. We help them cook a meal and we eat together. They like the rituals like we hold hands and say grace. It's like the Walton's. We bang a gong when the meals ready.

It's very hard to keep them pinned to the table during the meal because they're not used to sitting round and having a meal together. But I've learned an enormous amount about their lives and their culture, about what significance sharing a meal with people has and how it breaks down barriers. Simply sharing a meal with people. They've asked for things like saying prayers – they're not church kids – they like lighting candles, or little rituals, saying prayers.

Coming from a more middle-class background, a secure family environment, I've been pretty horrified – I've tried not to show it, how shocked I've been. Stories of violence, you know of families with several fathers all of who are absent. Siblings, all of different parents. It helps me to realise we've become disaffected and to see them as real human beings. There's no children with problems, there's families or adults with problems and they get put on to the kids growing up.

A lot of what I try to do, and we try to do as a church in this community, is to do things to try and break down that suspicion.

So we do things to meet the needs of the community without asking anything back. We run a film. We don't charge anything to come in. We run a free meal for people with drug and alcohol problems. We're not expecting them to come to church. People have said to me, 'well, shouldn't you make it a condition that they come to Sunday school or church?'.

We try and do a lot of things which from a faith point of view I'd say is reflected in what Jesus did which was to heal people and reach out to people on the edges of society.

I think the danger is if you try and get it to grow too much overnight you just do it superficially, you do it based on entertainment, it doesn't go any deeper.

It doesn't really go into relationships, the way people live their lives, changing what's unhealthy and what's destructive. That's much more important to me than church attendance."

Patricia Davies, 46, churchgoer. Photographed in Folkestone

A member of the United Reformed Church, Davies sought help from her local Methodist Church minister in Great Wakering after becoming depressed. Eventually, she complained to the church authorities about the lack of support from the minister. Davies has launched a website to offer advice to others neglected by the church.

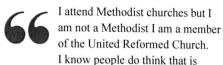 I attend Methodist churches but I am not a Methodist I am a member of the United Reformed Church.

I know people do think that is strange, I'm a member of one church but go to another. It is not strange because the URC is an ecumenical church. Its whole ethos is to join with other churches. So it is quite right that someone from the URC crosses the denominational boundaries. There is nothing happening in the URC, which I must say is typical of the United Reformed Churches. You won't find one open in the week.

My local Methodist Church I don't go to because of the problems. They are a Sunday club. They are a members only club. They don't function as a church. So, if you attend a church I don't recommend that you go there.

I candidated for the [URC] ordained ministry and that's when the trouble started. My mentor who was assigned to me had no experience, I don't think he had a clue what he was doing.

You think about the responsibility of mentoring a candidate for the ordained ministry... somebody who is going to minister parishes and churches. That's a responsibility. You need someone who knows what they're doing. And the Synod very naively gave me this prize prat who didn't have a clue. What he thought was that he had to mould me into him. Well, I don't want to be a prized prat so there was no way I was going to be moulded into him. He just tried cloning me. He even gave me words that I wasn't allowed to say which is absolute bollocks. There's another word I'm not allowed to say and I'll say it for that reason. But he's where all the trouble started. Him and the Methodist minister his friend, the one I put on the disciplinary.

I was studying for two years, a theology course and you had to have a support group. He was the convenor, the leader of my group. His methods were absolutely bizarre. It was supposed to be about the course, what I'm studying, that's what he was supposed to be supporting me on. But he turned it into constantly having a go at me personally. I went to a meeting, it was supposed to be about the course. How am I getting on with the course, what support do I need. If there's any problems doing the course. That was what the

support group was meant to be about. Another man opened up the group meeting and I can remember what he said to me, I can visualise him sitting down. He said, 'Pat I'm given the impression that you are on a short fuse. Can you give me an example of something that irritates you?'.

What's that got to do with the course? Apart from nothing. Why would he have got that impression? He'd been primed by the minister. When I challenged him they just fluffed and bumbled about. I got annoyed because the whole group was this sort of silly interrogation and then someone else said to me, 'how would you describe your listening skills?' As this was nothing to do with the course I was studying, theology, I remember slapping my hand on the arm of the chair and saying, 'a bloomin' sight better than yours'.

They couldn't even listen to what the course was about. That hadn't gone in. The minister lost his temper. 'I really do object to that comment, I find that offensive!', he said. So, I've got a short fuse? Look at this man. Then the other man said, 'look what you've done, you've made the minister prickly'. Never mind that they had made me prickly.

I asked the Methodist minister if she'd take over. She wasn't supportive at all. She would have a meeting with me where she seemed to be perfectly reasonable and perfectly supportive but she used to go sniding back to the minister. I then started to become ill. I suffered from depression many, many years ago. And I started to feel the symptoms creeping back. Naively she was the first person I went to.

This minister has got a ministry of healing, laying hands, prayer, prayers of healing. It's not sincere, can't be. Because what happened then was quite catastrophic. I'm suffering from depression, I'm no good. She started the abuse.

I went to work for the local hospice as a bereavement councillor. The first thing she did was to refuse a reference. I couldn't get in to the hospice and work for them without a reference and they accepted her as a referee. When they applied for it she said she knew nothing about it. Lied to them. That was a ghastly thing to do. Because not only did I lose

the placement I discovered something about her which gobsmacked me. The fact that she's a nasty piece of work. That was a really awful thing to do. It was damaging, it was hurtful.

But when we got to the hearing, the panel, I don't know how you would describe these quasi-judicial church or court hearings, their only agenda is to exonerate their own, no matter what she's done, and that's exactly what they did.

My depression was quite bad, it was getting serious. It was worsened by her. I think I would have recovered much quicker, much better, had a much more easy time of it if she'd have been supportive rather than vindictive. It was bad. I had five months without sleeping. Insomnia was chronic. I couldn't think straight. It's difficult to look back and think that anybody could be in that state and survive. It wasn't as severe as the first time in 1990 but it was bad.

She lied to them, I mean, what respect did she have for that church when she lies to them like she did? No, the church should not back her up. The church should be open to look at the reality of what's happened but they don't. I do not have any respect now for ministers of religion. I don't want to be one now, don't want to work with them. The church is closed. Basically, if you don't conform they give you a rough time.

It's not religion, it's not Christianity. The church is an outlet, it's a sink for people who have got nothing else to do. You find an awful lot of people in churches but you don't find many Christians and that's something I've come across in Great Wakering.

That's why the churches in Great Wakering are largely closing down. The Methodist Church has got a small, miniscule membership. The URC had a miniscule membership and it's shut now. The Catholic Church closed years ago. The Salvation Army closed. No, they are not thriving.

I want to find other people who have their voices silenced as aggressively as I have – bullied, victimised and harassed because if they do it to me they do it to 100 others. There are other people out there who have probably made complaints against ministers and, like I have been, threatened bullied and harassed to shut up. 99

Noem Oren, 16. Photographed in Hertzyla, north of Tel Aviv, Israel

In 1995 Oren's grandmother was killed by terrorist attack on a bus in Tel Aviv. He is a member of the Parents Circle – Families Forum organisation which aims to reconcile Israeli and Palestinian families who have lost family members in the long-running conflict.

"My grandmother died from a terrorist bomb in a bus in Tel Aviv 12 years ago. It was the intifada, there were a lot of attacks. The time was 1995. I didn't really get to know her in her old age. I was three. But I miss getting to get to know her. I have a few memories of her, the terrorists took the opportunity for me to get to know my grandma. I have shadow memories. Not really something big. Her face I remember, a family dinner.

After you have lost someone you understand the war only make wars. When you see the other side you come to the conclusion that you have to be tolerant to the other side.

It's a really complicated situation. I believe it was right for the Israeli army to occupy Palestine as a temporary solution. Because terrorists keep coming and Israel couldn't end this situation, because it's not like you are fighting with a country, it's individuals, so you can't blame Palestinians.

In order to avoid this situation of Palestinians coming from their lands and do terrorist attacks the army can occupy this land and got in. And now to get out you have to have a lot of security checks.

We don't have many terrorist attacks. It's worked. Sometimes it's happened, but when I was in 7th grade or 8th grade it was like everyday some people would die from terrorist attacks. It was really scary to go out. It also came to my city one time and there was panic. Everytime you wanted to go to a shop or a coffee house you had to have a security check to open your bag. Everyday. You really got used to it. Now we don't have terrorist attacks.

My problem with it is I see it as a temporary solution, we can't keep being there – the occupation. The attitude of me, I think, is different from most people. We have to realise how they [the Palestinians] live and I think most people don't do it. And most people don't remember this is a human being, and see them as enemies.

Each side thinks the other doesn't want peace because they don't know each other. Yes, I think this is really problematic. We can blame the media for most of this because we only see the false side. What you see in the news is a five-year-old Palestinian with a gun, Palestinian flag and saying, 'I want to be a soldier and kill Jews'. So you normally think, 'yeah, this is how they educated their children and they only want to kill us'. We don't understand that they have real people living there. For the Palestinians the only Israeli's they see is the soldiers. This is the Israeli image to them, someone who occupies them.

We don't really know what people think there. People think, 'they don't want peace, they want to kill us'. I think [we need] two countries or one country for both, as long as everybody, when saying their opinion, they have to keep in mind that we have to think of the other side every time.

I really think my opinion is the hardest approach, because I always have to think what the other person will think, how it will affect their life. People don't think like this because they think only about themselves. They want to live in Israel, they don't want someone to stop them in their country and they... I think they think of the Palestinians as numbers. I don't think it's really hard to be detached emotionally. I think it's really easy for a human being to ignore this humanitarian feeling and see them as enemies.

I can't hate someone by his race or his colour. This is how I was raised. I think my opinion obviously changed because I learned more. We have the same right to live here as them. We deserve to live here because we have no other place, this is the only place for the Jews. I don't say because there are other Arab countries they have somewhere else. The fact that there are countries with the same language and religion doesn't make it their country. They have the same right to live here as us.

When I see someone who I think is smart, normally I think he will think like me. How can a logical person or a sensitive person know all this pain that they are having and think differently than wanting to have peace? I don't say innocently I want peace. Some people say I am ignoring all the other facts and the political facts. But I can have a political argument about which lands should belong to us but it really doesn't matter. I think everybody should have the approach to see the other side all of the time. A lot of people in my classes look at them as animals. They don't want peace.

People think, 'I hate Palestinians now and you know that a Palestinian killed your grandmother, I would hate them ten times more'.

I don't want to negotiate with the Palestinians who killed my grandma, I hate them. They are murderers but you have to remember it's not all the Palestinians. It's really a low percentage of the Palestinians. We also have extreme cases in Israel of terrorists. Everybody can kill, it doesn't say anything about the Palestinians.

They think, 'if they want peace we want peace, but they don't want peace so I don't have to do anything'.

Some of my friends in Israel, they don't see the Palestinians as humans. People can have really closed emotions in this subject, I really don't get it sometimes. It's hard to see them as human beings and it's hard to want to negotiate with them.

But I think our organisation's approach is right, after we lost someone we understand that fighting won't do any good and we have to stop. And we have to stop this because we don't want anybody else to get to this conclusion like we did. After the grave.

I don't think my approach is an impossible mission. I try to convince people of my approach and I think it is possible. We can do it. It depends on both sides if they're going to approach the change.

I think I will be witness to peace because I think we were also close to that in the past and in time people won't stand for it if it's not getting better."

Shadi Abu-Awad, 17. Photographed in Beit Ummar, in the West Bank, Palestinian Territories

Two of Abu-Awad's uncles were killed by Iraqi soldiers in separate incidents. In 2000 Yosief, 32, was shot at point-blank range in Beit Ummar and in 2002 Saed, 16, was killed by sniper fire on his doorstep in Bethlehem.

" My uncle Yosief was driving his car to arrive in Hebron. At the checkpoint there were soldiers who dropped some little stones on his car. I don't know why they did that. So he stopped the car and asked the soldier why they do this.

The soldier asked him to get back in the car and stay in the car and not to say any word because if he does this, if he says anything, he will shoot him. So my uncle Yosief says, 'why, I didn't do anything I just ask you why you do this to me, why you drop these stones on my car?' So the soldier brings his gun and he put it to his face. My uncle shouted to him and asked him why and in a second he shot him in his head so his whole head exploded. It was terrible.

Saed, he lived in Bethlehem and I was there when he died. The Palestinian government and the Israeli soldiers were shooting. My uncle Saed was drinking tea. He went out to see what happened. He saw that people were still shooting so he came back. When he arrived at the door, they kill him, snipers. He was not in the middle, it wasn't that way. The soldiers want to kill him. They just kill him like that. I will never forget that. I just looked in shock. I didn't cry. I just looked.

I miss all of them and I miss everything about them. The most thing I miss about my uncle Yosief, when I did wrong things. I was throwing stones and rocks on Israeli cars. He told me that will not give us anything, that will cause a problem, it will not fix anything. So I miss his talking to me. And my uncle Saed. When he died I was ten or 11. He also took me to beautiful places. He was a very great uncle.

Mayed, my brother, two years ago they shot him in the leg. In seconds he will die, because they didn't have any blood. But the organisation [The Parents Circle] brought an ambulance and they took him to Israel to Hadassah and they saved him in the ambulance. He was close from death.

When the soldiers are in the village they start shooting. They come at three or four o'clock in the night and start shouting and destroying the door and want to search our house and wake all of us up. This is the other connection that is happening to us. Maybe once in two or three months. They go to the village and start

searching the houses. They came to our house maybe five or six times. They wake us up. Maybe sometimes they bring me and ask me questions, and try to hit me sometimes.

The first two or three years I was scared of the soldiers and the situation here. But now it is usual. Every night the soldiers go into the village shooting at something so it's usual.

In my mind I hated every Israeli in the world. And I would want to kill all of them. The soldiers, the people, children all of them. And that was in my head and I didn't think anything else.

But when you know this organisation Parents Circle we make contact between us and the Israelis and when we see what they say and what we say, I find that not all Israelis are bad. Israel, like here, there is good people who have no hand in the things that are happening here and also they lose people from their families. They lose, they say like me they want to stop this situation. They don't want to kill me. They didn't want to stop me going out of the house and put me in jail.

So when I see that, I understand that I shouldn't hate all the Israelis. And also, you know, I shouldn't hate anybody. I know I will die and also still hate the ones who killed my uncles and shoot my brother. I know I will not love the people who will do this anymore. But also I think that if you continue on the road of killing each other to win, nobody will win. They still kill us and we still kill them. Nobody will win.

I think that there's another road. I can win and he can win and not lose anything else. Because, actually, I'm not ready to lose anybody else from my family. If we can live together as Israeli and Palestinian together without killing each other we can make a connection, we can make a life because if the Israelis still say that we want the land and we still say that we want the land it will not finish it, it will stay forever. And we should finish this.

The first time they bring me and wanted me to sit with an Israeli in my mind I just know that they killed my uncles, they shot my brother they always wake us in the night and I wasn't ready to meet anybody.

But I sit down and I decided to listen and I

listened, and I understand what is really happening. Because I do not live in Israel, so I don't know what is happening. And also they sit down and listen and understand what is happening in Palestine because on TV they didn't see the truth.

So in that way our opinions was changed in seconds because when we hear what is happening there and understand the situation you will find that it is the same. So you shouldn't hate them, they didn't do anything to you. And also they shouldn't hate us because we didn't do anything to them.

I believe first of all that the soldiers should stop shooting and stop killing. And the second thing the soldiers – okay they are soldiers – but they are not soldiers to kill people, they are soldiers to protect their country, not to come to other countries and kill the people in it. So they should understand the job they should do. They should just protect their country. Maybe they should be in Israel to protect her. We have an army, a Palestinian government that can take care of us. So I think they should leave Palestine. Because this is our country and we should take care of ourselves.

Not all of my friends are ready to listen to me and understand me. You cannot tell them not to hate Israelis because you will not know what is happening to them. Maybe the mother, her son has died. Maybe the father, her sister, his mother, father, you cannot just go to him and say not to hate the Israeli. Let him tell us about what is happening to him. Tell us the sad thing, the sad time in his life. And we will bring anyone who is Israeli and tell them the same thing. That way we will understand each other.

I am sure we will have a peace because the situation will not stay like this. But if we have peace, and that is what they want, I think also it will stay a few problems. Because not all the Israeli people will understand peace and understand the Palestinian people and still hate us. And also some people of Palestine will still hate the Israelis.

The best way to have peace is to have a Palestinian state and also at the same time Israeli state and to have a connection, not everyone alone.

If we didn't have connection there would be no peace. "

Frans, 67, paedophile. Photographed in Deventer, The Netherlands

A husband, a father, a grandfather, a foster parent, a paedophile. Frans has had several sexual relationships with teenage boys. Though he still enjoys the company of children he has not had a sexual relationship with anyone under the age of consent for almost two decades. He is part of self-help group for paedophiles, JON, which aims to help those with strong sexual feelings for children control their emotions. Research found that as many as 25 percent of men have paedophile feelings, though the majority do not act on them.

" I have raised and cared for many foster children in the past, when I was married and after my divorce. I live alone here. Public opinion is once a paedophile, always a paedophile, for life – always dangerous – everyone who has feelings, sexual feelings for children, will always also act on them. That is the politically correct view. The most important thing is to make the differentiation between feelings and acts. Paedophile and paedosexual. It's a very great difference. If you don't accept this difference we cannot talk in a reasonable way. The public does not make this difference. They say all paedophiles are all the same. They say every paedophile is paedosexual. That is not true. There are lots of people with paedophile feelings who do not act on it.

People are able to change. Change themselves change their acts. It's very important. In the newspapers you read and hear always, 'oh, recidivism is very high'. This is not true. It is not, especially after treatment. They say recidivism is about 70 per cent. It's less, not more.

You can distinguish kinds of people with paedophile feelings in groups. Many of them do not allow themselves, any contact with any child any way. They withdraw from children. Other people, like me, have contacts with children, but have displanted themselves to keep also some distance. So, small but short contacts, not bodily. And surely not sexually. Other people have young friends. I know several people and they have young friends. They play with them they talk with them. But they avoid sexuality. And then a very small group does not avoid sexuality.

I had a short period with sexual contacts. I changed my mind after that – more than 20 years ago, several children. Some of them I had more intimate contact with, sometimes also sexual, male, around ten to 14 years old. Just after I split up with my wife. Exactly after that period. They were consensual.

Children search for love and intimacy. They need it and they feel it is possible. If they lodge at your home, they shower and sleep, it's a very short way to sexuality. It's around the corner.

Yes I have been prosecuted and convicted and sentenced. Five months. An accusation against me, 12 years later, when the boy was in his 20s and had lots of problems. Some of the children are adults now and don't express any complaint, does not tell [of] any harm.

If you have a doubt here inside you can put it under the table. Feelings of guilt. But doubts are irrational and sexual relationships are bodily and emotional, so two sides of the human way are in conflict.

Most people who have conscious paedophile feelings report that they have had such feelings from their childhood. The mean age of consciousness is nine years old. That's from a research report. Before the age of ten there is some confusion, maybe not a word for it, but there is a feeling for desire for contact with children, maybe desire for intimate sexual contact with children and the feelings of being attracted to youngsters. So it's early in life that it starts. So it must be, if not genetic, then developed in early childhood.

There came a younger child, maybe eight years. And then I thought I cannot combine this, it's not good. I have to stop. It's not good for him, not good for me. I have to try and retire myself, disview myself. He was always in my house. It was my opinion, my morality, my ethics. And society was changing around me. Especially in the eighties. In the midst of the eighties there was a switch in society. In the Netherlands about 1984, in Germany about 1987. There was a switch in public opinion in society and laws and general feelings about it. I have to live in this society, and when society changes I have to adapt.

The switch was too great. From tolerance to a very great intolerance. I reject behavourial therapy because it only concerns the behavioural outside of the human and not the inner side of the human. They neglect the inner side. The source is within you, not in your behaviour. But they want to control behaviour. Not good in my opinion.

People in their thirties and students join the group. They are in the age of seeking a partner and a lot of them in their life they see boy/girl, boy/girl, boy/girl, boy/girl. And their parents ask, 'do they have a girl? Did you meet a nice girl?' And they feel different. In their mind comes a kind of panic. They feel, 'I'm now on the wrong way'. And they feel frequently isolated. They withdraw themselves and then they come to the group. The group has been going for nearly 30 years. We have monthly talks and meetings. During the meetings people are asked to speak, 'I feel this, I have had this experience'. Paedophilia is not a dysfunction. A paedophile can very well do his job and family and finances and study and live quite good.

The feelings are not yours. Concerning the feelings, you have the choice: I accept them or I reject them. That is the conscious choice you have to make. Then I act on them or I do not act on them. And how to act or not to act. They are choices. But the feelings themselves they come up and they are there. You don't choose your feelings. You choose to accept them or not.

It's an inner process, self control. The way to conduct an obsession is first to accept yourself as you are. And that's what we do in the group. Talk with each other. We don't condemn each other, we don't convict each other. We accept each other. New members have to accept their feelings, have to accept themselves as they are. If you accept yourself you can proceed.

You have to realise that in the relationship sex is only a tiny part of it. Sex maybe only one or two or three times in five or six or seven years. So I don't regret relationships, only the sexual part of it.

My daughter knows everything of my feelings and relationships and conviction I have had. With my brothers and sisters I am as open as is possible.

A researcher in the United Kingdom was not allowed to publish [his report] because it tells about positive experiences and relationships between men and boys. That's forbidden to say.

If you suppress the feelings sooner or later the feelings will find a gate and burst. And then it's wrong. If you give room for your feelings, not all but a certain amount you can live more happier and without frustration.

I have sometimes some contacts with children but always short contacts and no bodily contacts and I can live. Now I walk with the dog and I see children I say hello and I walk off. And then I'm happy. Quite easy. Small contacts. I have learnt to keep the right distance, who is accepted by society. "

The End

All ages correct at time of interview.

Ken, speaker interviewed in 2008, Carl Makovecz, Reiki Master interviewed in 2009, Ivan Mackerle, treasure hunter interviewed in 2008, Brian Pattila, trainspotter interviewed in 2009, Nick Griffin, chairman of the British National Party interviewed in 2008, Yvonne Ridley, journalist interviewed in 2008, David Quincey, homeless interviewed in 2008, Sean Carr, lead singer, Death Valley Screamers interviewed in 2008, Jack Hughes, war veteran interviewed in 2008, Daniel Twiddy, Iraq war veteran interviewed in 2008, Ian, protestor interviewed in 2008, Queen's Guard interviewed in 2008, Sarah Batten, suffers from cerebral palsy interviewed in 2008, Mistress Sarah Kane, transgender dominatrix interviewed in 2008, Megan Phelps, student interviewed in 2008, Patricia Davies, churchgoer interviewed in 2008, Rev Andrew Allington, vicar interviewed in 2008, Noem Oren interviewed in 2008, Shadi Abu-Awad interviewed in 2008, Frans, paedophile interviewed in 2008.

Made in the USA
Middletown, DE
10 December 2015